Welcome to ...

100 Days With Jesus –
A Journey Through the Gospels

TOM HOLLIS

Enjoy your journey!

Copyright © 2021 Cornerstone Television

All rights reserved. No part of this book may be reproduced in any form or by any means, except for brief quotations in printed or online review, with the prior written permission of the publisher.

Published by CTVN Media, Wall PA.

Scripture quotations are taken from:

THE NEW INTERNATIONAL VERSION ®, (NIV)
© 1973, 1978, 1984, 2011 by Biblica, Inc.®
Used by permission. All rights reserved worldwide.

THE AUTHORIZED (KING JAMES) VERSION ®
Rights in the Authorized Version in the United Kingdom are vested in the Crown. Reproduced by permission of the Crown's patentee, Cambridge University Press.

The KING JAMES VERSION (KJV) ®
KING JAMES VERSION, public domain.

The NEW KING JAMES VERSION ®, (NKJV)
© 1982 by Thomas Nelson. Used by permission.
All rights reserved.

The ENGLISH STANDARD VERSION ®, (ESV)
© 2001 by Crossway, a publishing ministry of Good News Publishers. Used by permission. All rights reserved.

THE NEW AMERICAN STANDARD BIBLE ®, (NASB)
© 1960, 1971, 1977, 1995 by The Lockman Foundation.
Used by permission. All rights reserved. *www.lockman.org*

THE NEW LIVING TRANSLATION ®, (NLT)
© 1996, 2004, 2015 by Tyndale House Foundation.
Used by permission of Tyndale House Publishers,
Carol Stream, Illinois 60188. All rights reserved.

THE CONTEMPORARY ENGLISH VERSION ®, (CEV)
© 1991, 1992, 1995 by American Bible Society,
Used by Permission.

ISBN: 978-0-578-88906-1

Printed in USA

Dedication

*For Jean,
who has always walked with me
on this journey with Jesus.*

100 Days With Jesus

Introduction

*I*t was a long journey.

They had been walking with the Messiah for three years. Jesus had led them down many dusty roads and to many small towns, and even triumphantly through the gates of Jerusalem. He proclaimed the word of God before the small and the great.

And they were there for it all. The disciples had seen many signs and wonders. Jesus had performed mighty miracles; the blind could see and the lame walk! God was truly at work in this prophet from Galilee.

He had even sent them out with the same authority to heal and deliver. They rejoiced in the good work that God had given them the power to do. Jesus rejoiced too, even laughed, at the wonder of it all. But then He said a curious thing, *"Don't rejoice that the spirits are subject to you, rejoice that your names are written in heaven."*

With that statement, Jesus let the disciples know that there was something more important than signs and wonders. The highest joy in a disciple's life was to have a relationship with God through Christ. This is still the greatest joy for a Christian today.

In this small devotional, we have 100 days to spend in the presence of the same Savior. We get to walk alongside Him with Matthew, Mark, Luke, and John. They had left all to follow Jesus because He had the words of life.

A Journey Through The Gospels

You are on that same journey. As a Christ-follower, you get to walk with Him through the four gospels and see the same miracles. Better than that, though, you get to know Him. Jesus isn't a teacher who we study to be a little better in our lives. No. He is alive! And we get to walk with Him today in our towns and cities, and before the small and the great.

As you read each entry, you will find a corresponding chapter from one of the gospels. One day, one chapter. We spend more days in *The Sermon on the Mount* because there is just so much to learn there. For each chapter, I've written a devotional on one short passage, usually just one verse. It's the verse that happened to strike me that day.

On many days, I've written a little story. It's usually about what the biblical characters may have been thinking in that passage. Sometimes, I write a short story of how a modern disciple might apply the lesson of the day. I hope you enjoy them. That's one way God speaks to me.

God may speak to you differently. But God will speak! The relationship that Jesus had with the disciples is the same relationship that He wants with you now. I pray that as you read this devotional, you will grow in your love for Jesus and hear His voice clearly.

Let's begin the journey!

Tom Hollis

If you enjoy this devotional or have any questions or comments, I would love to hear from you. My email is thollis@ctvn.org.

100 Days With Jesus

Day 1
Matthew 1

God With Us

"Behold, the virgin shall be with child and shall bear a Son, and they shall call His name Immanuel," which translated means, "God with us." - Matthew 1:23

Just imagine what it must have been like to be Joseph. He was a good man, and he was looking forward to his upcoming marriage to Mary. He knew that she was a great "catch," and he was glad his parents had arranged such a good marriage. There would be joy and peace in their home with children soon to follow. He would teach them the words of God, the holy law given to Moses. It was going to be a great life!

But now this… Mary was pregnant. How humiliating! Joseph was really struggling. All his dreams of a life with Mary came crashing down. He was arranging to break up privately so she wouldn't be put to shame, but it hurt so much.

But last night he had a dream. Things were going to be all right. God had said so. But what was this child going to be? His name was going to mean, "God with us"? Joseph said quietly to himself, "Maybe our son is going to be a great prophet!"

We really can't blame Joseph for not fully grasping who Jesus would be. How could anyone know the child would be much

A Journey Through The Gospels

more than a prophet? He would be God incarnate, literally "God with flesh on." And yet he was also going to be born as a man.

Here is the beginning of a glorious mystery. Jesus was fully God and fully man … 100 percent and 100 percent. How is that possible? Only through God! There would be much anticipation as the child grew. Finally, His purpose would be revealed for all to see. He would conquer death, rise again, and save us from our sins.

Joseph's mind struggled to take it all in as he thought of the future. It was too much. For now, he had to concentrate on the wedding! "God is good," Joseph said.

We don't always know what's ahead of us. And though none of us will walk a road like Joseph, God will direct us. And like Joseph, we need to follow the path we are given, trusting in God the whole way. We are just beginning this Walk with Jesus!

Let's Pray:
God, thank you that Jesus lived among us.
Thank you Lord,
for beginning the journey in a carpenter's family.
Help me to hear your guidance just like Joseph did.
In Jesus' name, Amen!

100 Days With Jesus

Day 2
Matthew 2

WHERE'S THE KING?

Now after Jesus was born in Bethlehem of Judea in the days of Herod the king, behold, wise men from the East came to Jerusalem, saying, "Where is He who has been born King of the Jews? For we have seen His star in the East and have come to worship Him. - Matthew 2:1-2 (NKJV)

There was no doubt about it; they were lost. The three old astrologers from the east had come to Judea following the star they were sure proclaimed the birth of a new king. They had their expensive gifts with them. They wanted to honor the babe and worship Him. They weren't Jews, but they knew this child was someone special. Not just anyone got a star!

But now the star had disappeared, and they were unsure of where to turn. They wondered aloud; it seemed that no one among the Jews knew anything about the star or where the new king might reside. Well, since He is the king, then surely the palace would be the place to look. Herod received these distinguished visitors with honor, but his curiosity was piqued. Who were they looking for, and what did it all mean for him? He wasn't going to let some baby replace him, prophecy or not. Finally, the three wise men found the new king. The star had reappeared and led them to the exact place. It was a place they never would have looked: in the family of a poor carpenter.

"We Three Kings" had a misconception about the new king and

A Journey Through The Gospels

His kingdom. This was not going to be a king that dwelt in a palace. He wasn't going to have armies and wage wars. He wasn't going to have hundreds of servant; actually, He was coming to be a servant. He said so in Mark 10:45, *"For even the Son of Man did not come to be served, but to serve, and to give His life a ransom for many."*

Jesus' kingdom is so different: the first shall be last; low things will be exalted; the greatest is the servant of all. The magi got all this wrong, with some catastrophic consequences. Do we still get it wrong today? Are you a leader in the body of Christ? Then who will you serve today? Whose feet will you wash? Will you raise up those under you? This is the way of our King.

Let's Pray:
*Lord Jesus, you are my king. I live to serve you, and
I know that to serve you is to serve others.
Help me to be small in my own eyes today.
Help me to rejoice in lifting
up others. In your name, Amen!*

100 Days With Jesus

Day 3
Matthew 3

REVIVAL FIRES

In those days John the Baptist came, preaching in the wilderness of Judea and saying, "Repent, for the kingdom of heaven has come near."
- Matthew 3:1-2

The chapel was mostly empty, as the Wednesday night prayer meeting had concluded a few minutes ago. Most of the elders and pastoral staff were gone. Several people were talking, lingering around the sanctuary. Sheepishly, a young man approached the pulpit. The audio had been switched off, as had the podium lights. Still the young man walked to the pulpit. Weeping and passionate, he began to confess his sins. People were drawn to the front, dropping to their knees at the altar. Someone began singing. Soon another young person climbed into the pulpit to confess their sins. A musician seated himself at the piano and began to softly play. After two hours, the pastor and church leaders were called to come back to the church. Revival was breaking out!

The year of that revival was 1973, and it occurred in the campus church of Liberty University. This one service lasted until Saturday morning. It was four days of the continual move of the Holy Spirit! Classes were cancelled, people didn't go to work, or in many cases even eat. Some slept in the pews as the move of the Spirit ebbed and flowed. There were intense times of confession, and quiet prayer at other times.

A Journey Through The Gospels

Notice that the revival was birthed in a moment of repentance. This was the same ministry that was practiced by John the Baptist. Most of us say that we would like to see revival hit our church, but what does that really mean? We know that it has something to do with the fire of God and the move of the Holy Spirit, but how does it start?

Listen to John: *"I baptize you with water for repentance"* (Matthew 3:11a). Revival always starts with us. It starts in that place of repentance. Repentance is simply turning away from all known sin. Most historic revivals have started this way, including the humbling part of public confession. This acknowledges our total dependence upon God, when nothing matters but drawing close to Him. Repentance puts us in the right aspect to receive revival.

There is only one question: *Will we do it?*

Let's Pray:
God, I need to be revived. I need you to fill me afresh with your fire. I repent of my sins and trust in you for victory. Please move in might and power and burn up all the chaff in my life. I love you, Lord! Amen!

100 Days With Jesus

Day 4
Matthew 4

CALLING ALL FISHERMEN

While walking by the Sea of Galilee, he saw two brothers, Simon (who is called Peter) and Andrew his brother, casting a net into the sea, for they were fishermen. And he said to them, "Follow me, and I will make you fishers of men." Immediately they left their nets and followed him.
- Matthew 4:18-20 (ESV)

I'm not a great fisherman. Actually, that is an understatement; I am a lousy fisherman. If I had to feed my family by fishing, we would surely starve. When my kids were younger they were sad that I had never caught a fish. Never. Though we didn't do it often, one day we were fishing at a lake and I was, as usual, not catching anything. Ten-year-old Tiffany was having a problem with her rod, so I handed my rod to her younger sister Ashley, who wasn't fishing because she was only about five at the time. Immediately, Ashley caught a fish! I went the rest of that morning without a catch. Typical.

Jesus calls His first four disciples in this chapter, and they are all fishermen. Jesus made a little pun out of their profession. From now on they would be catching men. I wonder what they thought as they pondered that statement. How would they be catching people? Was this strange man a prophet? They weren't sure, but there was something magnetic about Him.

Jesus was really speaking about "catching" the souls of men.

A Journey Through The Gospels

He later stated the famous words of John 3:16 and adds verse 17 for good measure: *"For God so loved the world, that He gave His only Son, that whoever believes in Him should not perish but have eternal life. For God did not send His Son into the world to condemn the world, but in order that the world might be saved through Him."* (ESV)

Jesus knew His mission from the start, and called those to Him that they might be co-laborers with Him in the harvest of men's souls. That is still His call today. Let's not stay in the boat while He calls us to the world. And don't worry… you don't have to be a great fisherman. He will use your particular gifts to touch a life. Hey… even I eventually caught a fish! Really!

Let's Pray:
Lord Jesus, please let me heed your call today.
You are calling me to lost and hurting people
who need your love and need your salvation.
Help me to be a conduit of your love.
In your name, Amen!

100 Days With Jesus

Day 5
Matthew 5:1-12　　　　　　　　　　　　　*FIRST WORDS*

> *And seeing the multitudes, He went up on a mountain, and when He was seated His disciples came to Him. Then He opened His mouth and taught them, saying…*
> - Matthew 5:1-2 (NKJV)

We are going to be spending the next several days in the *Sermon on the Mount.* There is just so much to talk about here. We could easily spend a year in the next three chapters. I hope you like that as much as I do. Our God isn't shallow; He is a God of depth. His word has depth. We need to dig in, meditate on, wrestle with, and digest scripture. For several days we get to do that with the greatest sermon ever preached.

Here's Jesus, about to start the ministry for which He came to this earth. For thirty years, He has been waiting. He has been baptized by John, announced by the voice of God and tempted in the wilderness. He has called His first few disciples, and He has begun to preach repentance and do miracles. Now He is about to begin the greatest speech, the greatest teaching, the greatest sermon that has ever been spoken in world history: *The Sermon on The Mount.*

So how does He start? How would you start if you were Jesus? Would you tell everyone that you are the savior, that you are God in the flesh? Would you lay out the plan of salvation? Would

A Journey Through The Gospels

you tell them how much God loved them? Would you blast them for their sins? Would you start off with a funny story? (I might do that.) Jesus doesn't do any of that. He begins with, *"Blessed are the poor in spirit, for theirs is the kingdom of Heaven."*

Why do you think He begins with this phrase? Jesus is aware that we must be poor in spirit before we will reach for the richness of heaven. I have noticed while ministering in prisons, that prisoners have one advantage ... they know they are poor in spirit. They know they need a savior.

But what does that mean for us who already know Christ? It still is a time for us to realize our own inadequacy apart from Christ. Do you have a pain today, a need, a hurt? You are poor in spirit, and Jesus, in His opening line, offers you the kingdom of Heaven today, here on earth.

Let's Pray:
*Lord, thank you for saving me from myself.
Thank you for giving me access to the
kingdom of Heaven. I need that kingdom in
my life here and now.
I need you, Lord Jesus and all that you
have for me today. Meet me in my distress!
Thank you!
In your name, Amen.*

100 Days With Jesus

Day 6
Matthew 5:13-20 — LET IT SHINE!

> *"You are the light of the world.*
> *A city set on a hill cannot be hidden."*
> *- Matthew 5:13-20*

*L*ight of the World! What a great title for Jesus. I mean, He is the light, right? Scripture says, *"The people in darkness saw a great light!"* Jesus is the light. Or maybe we could use that title for God the Father. Yeah, *"God is light and in Him there is no darkness at all."* Yeah, it's about God.

But, wait a minute. That's not what Jesus is saying here. He is saying I am the light of the world. Me? Yeah, me. And you, too. That's a lot of responsibility, isn't it? I figure Jesus is great at shining a light on things. He can show God's love perfectly. But me, I get angry at the guy in the car in front of me for driving in the wrong lane. I get impatient with the slow checkout clerk. I'm not sure I'm really up to being the "light of the world."

Well, Jesus thinks I am. So, let's break this down. A light is something that shines, and it's something that can be seen. *Aren't you glad I'm giving you these great revelations?* So, if I'm meant to be the light of the world, that means that I have something inside of me that needs to shine on the people of the world. Of course, that light is God's love and truth, expressed in the gospel.

A Journey Through The Gospels

God made each of us unique. And as unique and distinct individuals, we each have a distinct role to fill as light of the world. Billy Graham certainly let his light shine for God, and we are glad he did. But you can reach someone that Billy Graham couldn't reach. You are the light of God for that person.

How do we do it? Show love. Be interested. Cut their grass. Smile. Pray. Tell them about God. In short, just BE the light of the world. Live the life right in front of your family, friends, neighbors and co-workers. Sometimes this type of ministry is referred to as "organic." Just be natural. Be who you are in Christ. This is the easiest and most authentic way to let your light shine.

Let's Pray:
God, you said I am the light of the world,
and you know what you are talking about.
So please help me let my light shine
to those all around me. Help me to touch
as many people as I can with your love.
In Jesus' name I pray, Amen!

100 Days With Jesus

Day 7
Matthew 5:21-26 — RIGHT RELATIONSHIPS

Therefore, if you bring your gift to the altar, and there remember that your brother has something against you, leave your gift there before the altar, and go your way. First be reconciled to your brother, and then come and offer your gift. - Matthew 5:23-24 (NKJV)

Uncle Wayne stepped up to the front of the church. I was nervous standing there in my white tuxedo. Next to me was the beautiful girl I was about to marry, holding a single red rose. To the right of me, and the left of her, were our faithful friends and family members. We stood before 150 witnesses who rejoiced to be there that day. Pastor Wayne, Jean's uncle, began his sermon on our wedding day, "Tom and Jean are people who believe in right relationships."

That's pretty much all I remember of Uncle Wayne's sermon that day. My mind was clearly elsewhere. But it has stuck with me all these years. You see, God is a God of right relationships. In our text, Jesus is speaking in His initial recorded sermon that we call the *Sermon on the Mount*. He uses the time to say a lot of radical things. One of the most radical is this ... He challenges the belief that you can be all right with God, but be at odds with your fellow humans.

But it strikes even deeper. Jesus is aware of the pharisaical idea

A Journey Through The Gospels

of God accepting mere religious observance, rituals designed to fulfill your check-off list with God. Jesus isn't impressed with that. He isn't after an outward show of religion while our heart is far from Him. No, God is real. And He wants real relationships between us. He wants whole people, healed people, in whole and healed relationships with one another.

So, what is our response today? Well it's pretty clear. Do you know a relationship that isn't right with someone? Do what you can to heal it. If you are at fault, even a little bit, then ask forgiveness. If you have been hurt, forgive the other person and seek to make it right.

God's kingdom is vertical and horizontal. To be in a proper relationship with our Father in heaven, we must seek that same type of relationship with our fellow man. It must be real. God isn't into check-off lists.

Let's Pray:
Father, let my heart be one of forgiveness and reconciliation. Never let me seek to serve you with wounded people in my wake. Let me say with the apostle Paul, "So far as it depends on you, be at peace with all men." Make a way, Lord.
In Jesus' name, Amen!

100 Days With Jesus

Day 8
Matthew 5:27-37   *Is Jesus Serious?*

"If your right eye causes you to sin, pluck it out and cast it from you; for it is more profitable for you that one of your members perish, than for your whole body to be cast into hell. And if your right hand causes you to sin, cut it off and cast it from you; for it is more profitable for you that one of your members perish, than for your whole body to be cast into hell."
- Matthew 5:29-30 (NKJV)

Sometimes it's hard to understand the difficult sayings of Jesus. Our text today is truly one of those. But here it is, right in the Sermon on the Mount. Jesus is telling us to tear out our eye and cut off our hand. What does he mean by that? Is He serious?

Throughout his ministry, Jesus would speak words that would bring life. Some are poetic, such as the Lord's Prayer. Others are harsh, "You brood of vipers!" Jesus was also not above using outrageous examples to make a point. Remember the camel through the eye of the needle? That was an outrageous, even comical, example. So is the beam in your eye. Nobody really had a 2 x 4 in their eye. Jesus was making a point. Well, here is another such outrageous example.

Is Jesus really telling you to get a hacksaw and take it to your hand? No. This is a metaphor. What He is doing is making a statement about how awful sin is. Sin is so bad that it will send

A Journey Through The Gospels

you to hell. If your eye causes you to sin, it would be better to be blind. If you can't control your hand, it would be better not to have one. Jesus wants everyone to make it to Heaven. Sin is so painful to us and to everyone around us. It would be better to lose our limbs than to stay in sin that will keep us from Heaven.

Sometimes a person gets into a pattern of sin that they just can't seem to break. I've told many people that they need to "throw a monkey wrench" into that sinful pattern. In other words, they need to do whatever it takes to get off the sin carousel. They need to desperately want victory. This is what Jesus means.

Let's Pray:
Holy God, you paid a high price for my sin.
It cost you the life of your only begotten Son.
Let me always take my sin seriously and give it
up completely. Give me your power and grace.
Thank you, Lord! Amen!

100 Days With Jesus

Day 9
Matthew 5:38-48

RADICAL

> *"You have heard that it was said, 'You shall love your neighbor and hate your enemy.' But I say to you, love your enemies, bless those who curse you, do good to those who hate you, and pray for those who spitefully use you and persecute you.* - Matthew 5:43-44 (NKJV)

The decade of the 1960's was a radical time in America. There were protests, even riots, over the Vietnam war and racial equality. It was a time of hippies, peace signs, cults, and communes. There were some in this counterculture who tried to adopt Jesus as the ultimate counterculture subversive, the first hippie, as it were. (His long hair helped.) There was a reaction from establishment Christians, in many ways a correct reaction, that Jesus was no Marxist-inspired radical. He was the nice tidy Savior that we learned about in Sunday School, wasn't He?

But Jesus is a radical! He was certainly a radical against the religious establishment of His day. He criticized the ways of the Pharisees, a lot. But in today's passage is another radical saying of Jesus with which we must wrestle, *"Love your enemies."*

He starts by saying that, up to this point, we've been told to hate our enemies. Who was saying that? The Old Testament never tells us to hate our enemies. In fact, we are told to love our enemies in Leviticus 19:18. So to what is Jesus referring? He is

A Journey Through The Gospels

addressing the popular misrepresentation of what God wants. He is attacking the teaching of anyone ... Pharisees, Sadducees, Romans ... anyone who has hate directed to their enemies. Love is the new and true commandment.

Can we really love our enemies, though? Jesus tells us to love and pray for our enemies. Perhaps that is the key. I'm not going to tell you that loving the unlovable is easy; it isn't. However, when we pray, we begin to get our heart aligned with God's heart and His purposes. The more time we spend with God, the more like Him we become.

But why does God want us to love our enemies? It's because He loves them. He wants them to be saved, healed, and delivered. After that, we will have far fewer enemies.

Let's Pray:
Lord, my enemies have hurt me and
I don't want to forgive them.
Part of me never wants to love them.
But you have forgiven me,
and I need to forgive and love.
Help me to have the love of God
in my heart always.
In Jesus' name, Amen!

100 Days With Jesus

Day 10
Matthew 6:1-15 — **PRAYER FROM THE HEART**

Pray, then, in this way: 'Our Father who is in heaven, Hallowed be Your name.' - Matthew 6:9

I stood in the pulpit of Calvary Baptist Church hearing prayer requests from the congregation. I was the visiting preacher and was about to pray for those requests. The deacons had also asked me to lead the congregation in the Lord's Prayer. I was nervous. All my life I learned the Lord's Prayer as I was taught it, especially this verse, *"Forgive us our trespasses as we forgive those who have trespassed against us."* However, I asked one of the deacons beforehand, and confirmed that Baptists say it this way, *"Forgive us our debts as we forgive our debtors."*

If you were brought up in the church like I was, you learned the Lord's Prayer by rote memorization. One Sunday School teacher after another taught it and prayed it. The whole congregation recited it every Sunday. After years of this type of usage, we had it memorized.

This always gives me pause, though. Is this what Jesus wanted? Jesus had just finished telling the crowd, *"And when you are praying, do not use meaningless repetition, as the Gentiles do."*

A Journey Through The Gospels

Now He gives them a prayer that has become for many, not all, a type of meaningless reciting, repeating the words without thinking about their meaning. This isn't what Jesus had in mind at all.

So, what is Jesus telling us to do when He shares this most famous of all prayers with us? He is giving us a guide for our prayers. He is letting us know what elements are important in our prayers. And most foundationally, God wants heartfelt prayers. He is not into memorization if it isn't backed up by the mind and heart of the person praying. God desires a relationship with us, and prayers that come out of that relationship.

Let's Pray:
*God, you are my heavenly Father. Let me always
stay close to you and feel your heartbeat.
Let all my prayers flow out of that closeness to you.
In Jesus' name, Amen!*

Back to my story: I was so nervous that day in the Baptist church that as I began to pray the Lord's Prayer, I messed up the second verse! I didn't even get to the "debtors" part before a misquote! What a great visiting preacher, NOT! When I was done I made a little joke about it. They were gracious, and it was a great service. *PTL!*

100 Days With Jesus

Day 11
Matthew 6:16-24   *SOGGY TREASURE*

"Do not store up for yourselves treasures on earth, where moth and rust destroy, and where thieves break in and steal." - Matthew 6:19

A national television audience watched in breathless anticipation as the safe was hauled up from the bottom of the ocean. A shipwreck had been searched, and a safe was discovered. A crane was brought in, and the heavy treasure chest was being slowly drawn to the surface. The host of the program gave everyone a play-by-play account of the events that could be plainly seen on the tv screen.

Finally, the heavy booty was laid to rest on the deck of a ship. Through various means, the door was removed. Here was the moment we'd all been waiting for! What was in this safe? Gold? Silver? Diamonds? Perhaps stock in Standard Oil. Surely some coins and folding money would be inside, right? Actually, as the door came off and water poured out, the safe revealed its contents ... paper ... insignificant, worthless paper. Soggy "treasure," indeed.

The above story really happened and it nicely illustrates a point. We will do all we can to protect our earthly treasures. Banks, guards, safes, alarms, insurance, or even burying it in the backyard.

A Journey Through The Gospels

Our treasures are precious to us. But earthly treasure is very tenuous. We can lose it all in an instant. Of course, we should be wise about protecting our assets. That is not the issue. The issue is, do we care more about our earthly possessions or our treasure in Heaven?

Jesus goes on to make it very clear to us what is really important: *But store up for yourselves treasures in Heaven, where neither moth nor rust destroys, and where thieves do not break in or steal; for where your treasure is, there your heart will be also* (Matthew 6:20-21). Heaven is what really matters. All our worldly possessions will pass away someday. But our treasure in Heaven will always be there.

How do we save heavenly treasure? Do the works of the kingdom. Live the life of Christ before the world. Give to those in need. Strengthen the weak. Serve the poor. Pray for those with a broken heart. In short, be a Christ-follower. Imitate Him and do his works, then we shall have treasure in Heaven. No safes needed!

Let's Pray:
Heavenly Father, you deserve all of me. Let my life be one of service in your kingdom. Give me strength to not just please myself, but to please your heart in all things. Make me effective for your kingdom today.
In Jesus' name, Amen!

100 Days With Jesus

Day 12
Matthew 6:25-34   *GOD'S VIEW*

"Look at the birds of the air, that they do not sow, nor reap nor gather into barns, and yet your heavenly Father feeds them. Are you not worth much more than they?" - Matthew 6:26

There is a business that exists today that wasn't around when I was a kid: self-storage facilities. Over the past thirty years or so, self-storage places have popped up everywhere. We Americans sure do love our stuff, don't we? I don't mean that we love individual things, I mean that we love having lots of stuff! Our closets are full; Our basements are packed; We can't get our car into the garage; It's tough to see the mower in our sheds. "What am I to do? Where else can I put my stuff?"

The storage industry arrives on the scene as your solution. For a monthly fee, you can store all of your extra things in a little mini-garage. There are even climate-controlled storage units so that our important collections of old clothes, old dishes, unopened gifts and mementos don't get overheated. We can sock them away and come visit them once a month, or once a year, or never. (Have you ever seen the show *Storage Wars*?)

There is nothing inherently evil in this, but it always struck me as the wrong focus. Why do we keep all that stuff? Why not just give it away? We have become so consumed with acquiring things that

A Journey Through The Gospels

we have overdone it. Television programs can be interesting cultural indicators. I've already mentioned *Storage Wars*, how about *Extreme Hoarders*? And now there is a reaction against acquiring stuff with the *Tiny House* program and the minimalist movement among young people. We just love to swing to extremes.

God has a different view: He wants us to trust Him. Inside of the desire to keep our stuff lives a trust issue. Do we trust God to provide for us? Even with prosperity, we are seeing elevated levels of anxiety. Jesus has a cure for that:

But seek first His kingdom and His righteousness, and all these things will be added to you. So do not worry about tomorrow; for tomorrow will care for itself. Each day has enough trouble of its own (Matthew 6:33-34).

It's natural for us to worry. It's normal to want to provide a defense against any calamity. But the true answer is not in our stuff. When we seek God's kingdom, He gives us all we need.

Let's Pray:
Lord, let me always put your kingdom ahead of my own kingdom. Let me not be anxious for tomorrow. You hold all my tomorrows in the palm of your hand. Let me not take comfort in my possessions, but instead always trust in your faithfulness.

100 Days With Jesus

Day 13
Matthew 7:1-12

LOGS AND SPECKS

"Or how can you say to your brother, 'Let me take the speck out of your eye,' and behold, the log is in your own eye?" - Matthew 7:4

We live in judgmental times. Everyone has an opinion about something and they are more than willing to share it. Civility takes a back seat to expression. "Courage" to speak comes from the anonymity of the internet. Emails, voicemails, even our friends on Facebook will lash out with a strongly worded opinion on our conduct and beliefs.

In our text today, Jesus speaks out against judgmentalism. He tells us to remove the log out of our own eye. What does that mean? Jesus is calling us to examine our own thoughts, motives, and actions. He uses one of my favorite ways of speaking: the humorous metaphor. No one in the crowd that day actually had a hunk of wood in their eye, but everyone had a problem with judgmentalism. It's something that we humans do best.

How easy it is for us to ignore our own faults. Have you ever heard a sermon and wished that so-and-so would hear it? It's so much easier for us to see the problems in others, but God wants us to look inside ourselves first. Eighteenth-century evangelist John Wesley put it this way, "We should be gracious in judging others

A Journey Through The Gospels

and diligent in judging ourselves." That's the key. Examine our own heart. Examine our own eyes. Any logs in there? By the way, one thing about logs is they are BIG. Jesus is telling us that we won't have to look too long and hard before we see our own troubles for which we need repentance.

One side issue here: People always say that Jesus is saying not to judge. That's not exactly the case. Jesus is not telling us to accept everything. It is okay to have discernment. He even says that it is okay to take the "speck" out of your brother's eye. Jesus is warning against an attitude of the heart. Again, grace will help us here, as well as keeping things in proper order.

Let's Pray:
Dear Lord, keep me humble and gentle.
Keep me far from the judgmentalism of this age.
Let me always view others with the eyes of grace.
Show me my own heart and help me to remove
those things which displease you.
In Jesus' name, Amen!

100 Days With Jesus

Day 14
Matthew 7:13-23

GATES

"Enter by the narrow gate; for the gate is wide, and the way is broad that leads to destruction, and many are those who enter by it. For the gate is small and the way is narrow that leads to life, and few are those that find it." - Matthew 7:13-14 (NAS)

I remember an old Twilight Zone episode where a country grandpa was hunting with his hound dog. Something happens, and he finds himself in an unknown area that just so happens to be the gateway to the afterlife. He realizes that he is dead, though his faithful hound is still with him. He approaches a gateway where he is greeted by a pompous gatekeeper. The man is all about rules and regulations. He tells him that this is the gateway to Heaven. He gives the grandpa a hard time and says that his dog can't come in. Taking exception, the grandpa says, "If he can't come in, I'm not going in." He walks away down the road to the shouts of the gatekeeper telling him not to go that way.

In a little while, the grandpa comes upon a man in jeans and a flannel shirt. He has a down-home accent and invites the grandpa to the cook-out that is just getting started. It's just down the road a piece, and he is more than welcome. The old man pauses for a bit and asks if his hound dog can come. "Sure," says the stranger, "bring him along!" They head down the road and pass into glory.

A Journey Through The Gospels

We can easily be deceived in this life. As we travel the road, there are many temptations to turn off the way God has laid out for us. We can be tempted to sin or compromise our faith. Or we can just get distracted away from the things that really matter. Jesus called it the "cares of this life." They pull us off course, make our engine overheat, and give us a spiritual flat tire. Our spiritual enemy will do anything he can to distract us from the straight and narrow way.

Most people don't even find the narrow gate. They are completely oblivious to which road they are on. Jesus said that this gate is wide and the way is broad that leads to destruction. Many of our friends and family are on that road.

So, why does Jesus tell us this? First, He wants us to be on the right road ourselves. We won't have our hound dog with us to show us the way. Second, He wants us to remember that we need to warn those who are on the wrong road. He has entrusted that gospel message to us. Think about everyone you see out on the street, in the grocery store, or a Pirates' baseball game. A majority of them are on the way of destruction. Help them to find the narrow way. Maybe you should invite them to a barbeque!

Let's Pray:
Lord, help me to live my life with eternity in view.
You desire everyone to be saved, but many need to
hear the gospel. Make me your messenger today.
In Jesus' name, Amen.

100 Days With Jesus

Day 15
Matthew 7:24-29

FOUNDATION WORDS

"Therefore, everyone who hears these words of Mine, and acts upon them may be compared to a wise man, who built his house upon the rock." - Matthew 7:24 (NAS)

Pittsburgh (my hometown) is an unusual American city in that it is built on and around hillsides. One only needs to look up in any old Pittsburgh neighborhood to see houses precariously perched on the sides of hills and mountain bluffs. Though I have lived in the area for most of my life, even I am amazed at some of the places where houses have been built. But Pittsburgh builders have become very good at building strong foundations and anchoring them to the hillsides. The roads up to these houses can be steep, but the views are always spectacular.

Sometimes it doesn't work out though. Snow and rain are a never-ending battle on these hills. Earlier this year there was a lot of rain, and there was an astonishing video of a house actually sliding down the hillside!

Jesus tells us to build our house upon the rock. He says the strong foundation is made up of his words. He begins this sentence with "therefore," which means He is referring to what He just said. What He just said was *The Sermon on The Mount*. So, what is Jesus getting at? Just this: it is important that we not only hear the words

A Journey Through The Gospels

of Jesus, but that we act upon them. Acting on His words requires a change in us, and therefore is uncomfortable, but is the only way we can be built on the rock.

Recently, I began watching YouTube videos of a contractor building a brand-new house. He has been at it for a while now, and so far, he has not nailed one board to another. It has all been about site preparation and foundation building. The funny thing about a house is it can look beautiful on the top, but if the foundation is compromised, it is unfit and unsafe to live in. The same is true for us. We can say the right words and sing loudly on Sundays, but if our foundation is weak, we are in a dangerous position. We need to rebuild. We do that by following the words of Jesus. *The Sermon on the Mount* is a great place to start!

Let's Pray:
*Lord, I want to build my house upon the bedrock
of your words. Show me where my foundation is weak
and give me the bricks and mortar of your word to repair
and rebuild. When the storms come into my life,
let me know that my house will stand! Amen!*

100 Days With Jesus

Day 16
Matthew 8:1-17

INCREDIBLE POWER,
INCREDIBLE PROMISE

And He said to them, "Be gone!" And they came out and went into the swine, and behold, the whole herd rushed down the steep bank into the sea and perished in the waters. - Matthew 8:32 (NAS)

*D*eliverance as a ministry has always puzzled me. I've been in services where people have prayed for deliverance, and I've seen some glorious things happen. Other times, I've seen nothing happen, and the person seems to go away in the same state as before. I've always wondered why. I've heard explanations like, "They weren't ready to be delivered" or "They have to really want it." This doesn't seem to square with the biblical examples of deliverance given by Jesus.

Just look at our text today. If you read the last few verses of Matthew 8, you will see that there were two men who were so demon-possessed that they were violent and threatening. People couldn't even walk past them without being harmed. When they saw Jesus, they recognized who He was. Think about that for a moment. Demons are fallen angels. Therefore, Jesus knew these demons before they fell. He remembered them when they were good. They even asked Him to have compassion and send them into the swine, and He did. Immediately they left the men and went into the swine. The swine went mad and killed themselves.

A Journey Through The Gospels

Look at the incredible power Jesus demonstrates. These two men weren't "ready" to be delivered. They didn't even ask to be delivered. But the power of God is so much stronger than the enemy's power that the men were set free that day! It was glorious and sudden. As we minister the precious gospel of Jesus Christ, we will have His power. He made this incredible promise to us:

"Truly, truly, I say to you, he who believes in Me, the works that I do, he will do also; and greater works than these he will do; because I go to the Father" (John 14:12).

I want to do those "greater works." I want to see that power working in the lives of people God brings my way. I want herds of pigs to get nervous when I walk by!☺ And guess what? I have that power already, and so do you!

Let's Pray:
Lord Jesus, I know there are people nearby who need deliverance. They need to know your love, and they need to be set free. You said that I would have power and do great works. Give me the opportunity and the confidence in you to see miracles happen today.
In your name I pray, Amen!

100 Days With Jesus

Day 17
Matthew 8:18-34

SEE YA' LATER, LORD

The herdsmen ran away, and went to the city and reported everything, including what had happened to the demoniacs. - Matthew 8:33

*L*ast time, we talked about Jesus bringing great deliverance to two demon-possessed men. We shared that He has given us the same delivering power. But there is one more small part of this story that I just can't leave until we deal with it: the reaction of the townspeople.

As you can see from our text, the herdsmen, who had just lost a lot of pigs, went straight into the city and told everyone what had happened. They were probably glad to have the demoniacs delivered. At least they wouldn't harass them on the road any longer. But that gladness was turned around in a few seconds when their pigs ran over a cliff. These herdsmen were probably frightened and felt they needed people in higher authority to deal with Jesus. The city leaders came out and here is what happened:

And behold, the whole city came out to meet Jesus; and when they saw Him, they implored Him to leave their region (Matthew 8:34).

There are a few important things we can glean from this episode. First, when Jesus shows up, things change. Jesus never came for the status quo. Any time Jesus appears on the scene, He brings

A Journey Through The Gospels

changes. Secondly, Jesus brings judgment on our sin. Did you notice the animals the herdsmen were tending? Pigs. Jews were not to eat pork, so why were they herding pigs? They had fallen away from their obedience to God, and Jesus was calling them to account for it.

Finally, the whole city asked Him to leave. Wait a minute. Didn't they want deliverance? Didn't they realize that this was the Son of God they were telling to leave? Probably not, but they knew that He was a prophet, at least. And they didn't want Him messing with their lives. He was *persona non grata*. So, the Messiah, for whom they had waited all their lives, was sent packing.

What is the lesson for us? The lesson is in how we treat Jesus ourselves. When the Son of God comes calling do we embrace Him? "Of course," you say. What if He comes with conviction, do we embrace Him then? What if He wants to change our entire way of life? Will we embrace Him then? I hope so, because that's exactly how He is coming.

Let's Pray:
Jesus, I acknowledge that you are God and you are Lord. You are the one who changes everything. Help me to always be open to your will. Change me, Lord! Amen!

100 Days With Jesus

Day 18
Matthew 9

SACRED HEART

And seeing the multitudes, He felt compassion for them, because they were distressed and downcast like sheep without a shepherd.
- Matthew 9:36

Thaddaeus couldn't take much more of this. He could see Jesus, now far away as the crowds had pushed and jostled their way past him in an attempt to get closer. This had been going on for hours. One lame person, blind man, or leper after another coming to Jesus to be healed. He saw Jesus laying hands on so many, healing them all. "How long can He keep this up?" he thought to himself. Thaddaeus loved Jesus, but he struggled to care about these people. They were all so wretched. Are we ever going to minister in the palace? We need to see Jesus take his rightful place as king!

As he was wrestling with these thoughts and jostling with some more people, Thaddaeus caught sight of Jesus' eyes. He saw deep wells of compassion in those eyes. He saw Jesus' care and concern for the lowest and the least. Here was Jesus (*a prophet? the Messiah? Thaddaeus wasn't sure yet*) having compassion for people who had nothing. As Jesus turned to yet another person who needed a touch of God's love, Thaddaeus realized that Jesus was in exactly the right place. Here was a King who loved his people.

A Journey Through The Gospels

The disciples had a front row seat to everything Jesus did. What must it have been like to see the Son of God expressing the heart of the Father to these people? What must it have been like to be one of those people! To them, the Pharisees had always seemed distant. They were supposed to be the shepherds, but Jesus said that the people were like sheep without a shepherd. The priests were not fulfilling their duties properly.

The word "downcast" can also be translated as "harassed" or "thrown down." I don't know if you ever feel like that, but I know I do. The world, the flesh, and the devil can harass us and throw us down. Jesus lifts us up. And after He lifts us up, He gives us a part in lifting up others. Look at the very next passage, *Then He said to His disciples, "The harvest is plentiful, but the workers are few. Therefore beseech the Lord of the harvest to send out workers into His harvest"* (Matthew 9:37-38).

Today is a new day! If you are down, Jesus will have compassion. Then, see the people as Jesus sees them, and lift one up.

Let's Pray:
Lord, thank you for your compassion and grace.
Thank you for your love. Thank you for picking me up,
forgiving me, and healing me. Now make me an
instrument of compassion for others.
In Jesus' name, Amen!

100 Days With Jesus

Day 19
Matthew 10 —— *GOOD PREACHING*

And as you go, preach, saying, "The kingdom of Heaven is at hand."
- Matthew 10:7

It's important to pay attention to what the New Testament preachers did when they went out to preach. Sometimes it is far different than what we preach. If I was sent out to preach, I would tell the people everything about God's love and His salvation. I would speak of each person's sinfulness before God and how Jesus' sacrificial death on the cross gives us access to God's forgiveness. I would share that God is our Father who wants a relationship with His children. While I know these truths are biblical, it is not what was always shared by the apostles.

When Jesus sends out the apostles, he tells them to say, "the kingdom of Heaven is at hand." What did this mean to a Jew of the first century? Well, a kingdom has a king. I'm sure to them it stirred thoughts of the king and messiah who was to come. The promised savior that they had waited for … was he really here?! This would have roused the interest of everyone. Of course, the religious establishment almost always rejected their message. What does it say about religious people when the most religious people are the ones who totally rejected this preaching?

A Journey Through The Gospels

There is a passage in First Corinthians 2:4-5 that stirs me, *"And my message and my preaching were not in persuasive words of wisdom, but in demonstration of the Spirit and of power, so that your faith would not rest on the wisdom of men, but on the power of God."* This is such an important point: our gospel is not a gospel of words but of power! Perhaps another way of saying this might be, our gospel is not just words. The apostles were not just told what to say, they were given authority to work miracles. Jesus told them, *"Heal the sick, raise the dead, cleanse the lepers, cast out demons. Freely you received, freely give"* (Matthew 10:8). Now that is some power!

So where does that leave us? We have the same message and the same power. All we need to do is use it. If we preach the gospel, the signs will follow. Take a step today and see what God does!

Let's Pray:
Heavenly Father, how easy it is for me to forget the awesome power you have given us. Please use me today to touch a life with the words and power of the gospel. In Jesus' name, Amen!

100 Days With Jesus

Day 20
Matthew 11

Cabin Rest

"Come to Me, all who are weary and heavy-laden, and I will give you rest." - Matthew 11:28

My family takes two very different types of vacations. I'm sure many of you will identify with one or the other. First is what I'll call the "Disney World Vacation." This trip is nonstop action. It is one rollercoaster ride after another. It is filled with fun and people, lots of people. You rise before dawn and go, go, go until midnight. When you get back home, you need a vacation to recover from your vacation. I love this kind of vacation.

The second vacation is the "Cabin-at-the-Lake Vacation." Jean's uncle has a cabin on a lake in northern Iowa. We have gone there often. You rise early and go down to the dock to watch the sun come up over the lake. Then you go down to the general store to get your coffee, in which you pay whatever you want into a cast iron piggy bank and just walk out. You can ride a bike around the lake, but make sure you stop for ice cream in town. While you enjoy your cone, just sit in the shade and look at the lake. After dinner you can watch the sunset over the lake. I really LOVE this kind of vacation!

The second kind of vacation seems much more restful, doesn't it?

A Journey Through The Gospels

We were created to rest. What does it say about God that He has created us to need rest? He didn't have to do that, you know. He could have made us in a way that we could work all day. He could have given us two suns, so that it was always daytime. He could have put Adam and Eve in the "Factory of Eden" instead of a garden. But no. He created sleep and night and mealtimes and Sabbaths and holidays. He doesn't want productive servants so much as He wants children who love to be with Him.

In our text, Jesus calls to those who need rest, *"Come to me."* He knows we need it, and that we don't often get it. This is not the rest of a vacation, but a spiritual (and physical) rest for our souls. It is a rest we can know right in the middle of the stresses of life. Listen to Him as he continues, *"Take My yoke upon you and learn from Me, for I am gentle and humble in heart, and you will find rest for your souls. For My yoke is easy and My burden is light."* (Matthew 11: 29-30).

Let's Pray:
Father, let me remember that my highest calling is not to be busy, but to know you. Help me to take your yoke upon myself. It is a yoke of freedom. Let me experience the freedom and rest that is part of my inheritance as a child of God.
In Jesus' name, Amen.

100 Days With Jesus

Day 21
Matthew 12   COMPASSION, NOT SACRIFICE

For the Son of Man is Lord of the Sabbath. - Matthew 12:8

Jesus was walking in the fields. His disciples began to get hungry. What to do? *Chick-fil-A* wouldn't open for another 1,934 years. So, they began to pick heads of wheat and eat the grain. Not so filling, but better than nothing. The Pharisees saw this (what were they doing out there anyway?) and rebuked them for doing what was not lawful on the Sabbath. This gave Jesus an opportunity to say some amazing things.

Jesus, as he often did, answered their question with a question. He answered, *"Haven't you read what David did when he and his companions were hungry? He entered the house of God, and he and his companions ate the consecrated bread — which was not lawful for them to do, but only for the priests."* (Matthew 12: 3-4, NIV). This is an absolutely astounding thing to say to the Pharisees, and it even sounds strange to us. Picking grains of wheat on the Sabbath wasn't really against the Law of Moses but most likely was a religious add-on by the Pharisees. But what David did WAS definitely a violation of the scriptural law. What is Jesus saying? Is He saying don't worry about all that "law" stuff? No.

A Journey Through The Gospels

This is a chance for Jesus to teach the Pharisees, His disciples, and us, that what God is really after are matters of the heart. Nobody has ever been better at outward appearance than the Pharisees. They were world champions at it. How much must it have irked Jesus to see their superficial spirituality! He knew what was inside of them: hatred, jealously, greed, dead-men's bones. But they sure looked shiny on the outside.

Jesus wraps this segment up by saying two things. First, he tells them that He desires compassion and not sacrifice. The funny thing about we humans is we're always trying to make a religion out of everything. We want a to-do list that we can feel good about completing. We want to sacrifice for God, but He wants compassion from the heart. Second, Jesus gives the Pharisees a "mic drop" moment, *"For the Son of Man is Lord of the Sabbath."* Boom! ("Just in case you guys don't really know who I AM!") He is not just a prophet, He is God in the flesh.

Let's serve Him from the heart today.

Let's Pray:
Jesus, I confess that I am too often concerned with the outward appearance of myself and others. Help me to see people as you see them. Help me to see the person who needs your compassion and help me to be your ambassador of compassion to them. Amen!

100 Days With Jesus

Day 22
Matthew 13

Hidden Treasure

"The kingdom of heaven is like treasure hidden in a field. When a man found it, he hid it again, and then in his joy went and sold all he had and bought that field." - Matthew 13:44 (NIV)

Have you ever watched *Antiques Roadshow* on PBS? The basis of the program is to ask people to bring an antique, painting, memorabilia, or curiosity they own to be appraised by the experts on the show. Most of the time the antique is worth more than the owner expected. I'm sure many are not worth much, but those rarely make it on the show. Once in a great while a true treasure is found.

I remember one such instance several years ago. A woman brought in a side table done in a colonial style. She had paid $25 for it. The appraisers looked it over and pronounced it a rare and desirable table from the early American colonial period. They said at an auction that it would be worth in the range of $250,000! A few months later, the table did indeed go to auction. When the gavel was sounded, the final bid had come in at $435,000!! For years this woman had walked past her $25 table never knowing the riches it held.

In our text today, Jesus tells us that the kingdom of Heaven is a treasure. It is so great a treasure that it is worth selling all we have to buy it. Just for good measure He uses a second parable right

A Journey Through The Gospels

away that emphasizes the point, *"Again, the kingdom of Heaven is like a merchant looking for fine pearls. When he found one of great value, he went away and sold everything he had and bought it"* (Matthew 13:45-46, NIV). We know that we can't buy our way into Heaven, so what is Jesus saying? He is saying to obtain entrance into the kingdom will cost us all we have, and it is worth it. When we come to Christ, we must lay down our lives before Him. That is why we call Him *Lord*.

When the lady in the story above was considering purchasing the table, what would have happened if the price had been $150,000? Would she have sold her house and car to buy it? No, but it would have been worth it. How much more is entrance into God's kingdom worth?

Let's Pray:
*Lord, thank you for my entrance into your kingdom.
You laid your life down for me. You are truly the
pearl of great price. Obtaining you is worth any cost.
Help me to never take you for granted.
In Jesus' name I pray, Amen!*

100 Days With Jesus

Day 23
Matthew 14

HE WILL MAKE A WAY

> *But Jesus said to them, "They do not need to go away; you give them something to eat!"* -Matthew 14:16

*D*o you ever offer God your advice? I know I do. My prayer life can be filled with what I think is the best course of action for my Heavenly Father to take. I mean, if God would just do what I'm suggesting, everything would be great!

Quite often my suggestions to God are good. At least I think so! I'm sure I pray selfishly, too, but mostly I'm praying what I think are good things for everyone involved. In our passage today, the disciples had a good idea, and it was rooted in concern for others. Look at verse 15, *When it was evening, the disciples came to Him and said, "This place is desolate and the hour is already late; so send the crowds away, that they may go into the villages and buy food for themselves."* The disciples saw the people hungry and needing food. It was a compassionate motivation causing them to say this to Jesus. They thought, and here we come to the focal point of the matter, that it would be a great idea to let the people go get some food.

Human wisdom can be a wonderful thing. Common sense, insight, and good counsel can come from people who have experienced

A Journey Through The Gospels

life and learned many important lessons. I've benefited from the wisdom of many good people. But human wisdom can only go so far. It cannot see the miraculous. We serve a God who says, *"For My thoughts are not your thoughts, neither are my ways your ways"* (Isaiah 55:8, NIV).

We all know what comes next in the scenario with the multitudes. Jesus takes a little bit of bread and fish and feeds everybody. No human wisdom could foresee this. No amount of insight and planning and money could have provided for the multitude. But like the song says, "God can make a way where there seems to be no way." God not only sees things differently, he has the unlimited power to perform miracles.

Do you need a miracle today? Do you see nothing but roadblocks on the way to your answer? Realize God has answers you don't see yet. He can part the Red Sea or feed the 5,000. He can make a way for you!

Let's Pray:
God, let me always remember you see things differently than me. Help me to get your perspective on my situation, but even more, help me to trust in your love. You are not limited in any way. I know that you will make a way! In Jesus' name, Amen!

100 Days With Jesus

Day 24
Matthew 15 *WHAT IS JESUS DOING?*

And a Canaanite woman from that region came out and began to cry out, saying, "Have mercy on me, Lord, Son of David; my daughter is cruelly demon-possessed." But He did not answer her a word. - Matthew 15:22-23a

Sometimes I can really feel for the disciples. They had a hard job understanding what Jesus was doing and saying. Jesus doesn't always fit into a nice neat little box of what I think He should do or say, either. In our chapter in Matthew today, we have one of the more difficult scenes for me to understand.

Jesus is walking with the disciples, and as happened many times, He is confronted by someone who needs a miracle. A woman is asking for mercy for her daughter. Surely, Jesus will feel compassion. Surely, He will perform a mighty healing right away. Ummm... no. He first ignores her and then tells her, *"I was sent only to the lost sheep of the house of Israel."* He basically says that He can't help her, "It's not my department. I'm only here for Israelite folks." She is a very persistent person, however, and she keeps after Jesus. She falls at His feet and cries out in anguish, "Lord, help me!" I KNOW Jesus will help her, now!

Nope. Instead He says a line that I have a hard time even fitting into my concept of Jesus, *"It is not good to take the children's bread and throw it to the dogs."* What? How can Jesus be so callous? If

A Journey Through The Gospels

you prayed to God for a miracle, and you heard a voice coming out of heaven that said, "We don't give our stuff to dogs!" what would you do? You'd be crushed! You'd change religions or start rooting for the Baltimore Ravens! (Steeler fan here.) But this is exactly what Jesus says to her. She is undaunted. She comes back and asks again, for the crumbs. Finally, Jesus relents, and joyously says, *"O woman, your faith is great; be it done for you as you wish."*

So, what was Jesus teaching us through this scenario? First, no one is a dog. Jesus was trying to draw out her faith and doing it for all of Israel to see. Second, sometimes the heavens are brass. At times it seems like God isn't listening, but He is. Third, keep asking. Don't give up! The answer is on its way.

Let's Pray:
Heavenly Father, help me to anchor my faith in your love, especially when I don't see the answer as quickly as I would like. I trust you, even the crumbs from the children's table are enough to satisfy my every need. I love you, Lord! In Jesus' name, Amen!

100 Days With Jesus

Day 25
Matthew 16   *SIGN, SIGN, EVERYWHERE A SIGN*

And the Pharisees and Sadducees came up, and testing Him asked Him to show a sign from heaven. - Matthew 16:1 (NAS)

The Pharisees and Sadducees were quite a piece of work. Each group hated the other, but they were in unity in their denunciation of Jesus. They were also a proud bunch. They had the worst kind of pride that afflicts the human race: spiritual pride. They also had supreme confidence in their knowledge of God and always thought they could outwit this bumpkin prophet from Nazareth.

Jesus was busy. His appointment calendar was "full up." Just in the last two chapters of Matthew, He had fed the 5,000, fed the 4,000, healed multitudes and… oh yeah, walked on water. He was performing miracles at an astonishing rate. Remember when John the Baptist's disciples asked Jesus if He was the Messiah. What did Jesus say to them? *"Go and report to John what you hear and see: the blind receive sight and the lame walk, the lepers are cleansed and the deaf hear, the dead are raised up, and the poor have the gospel preached to them"* (Matthew 11:4b,5). Jesus was saying he was doing things the Messiah was supposed to do. His miracles were proof of who He was.

A Journey Through The Gospels

The Pharisees and Sadducees saw all of this. They tried to discount some of it, but they couldn't discredit it all. There were signs happening everywhere, and yet in our opening scripture today, they asked Jesus for a sign! These religious folks were great examples of those who will not believe, even if the evidence is right in front of them.

Jesus is having none of it. He says, "*An evil and adulterous generation seeks after a sign, but no sign will be given it except the sign of Jonah*" (Matthew 16:4, ESV).

The sign of Jonah is the resurrection. Jonah was in the great fish for three days and then set free. Jesus would be dead for three days and then raise to life. That is the greatest sign of all. Guess what? The Pharisees and Sadducees wouldn't even believe in Him then. God have mercy!

Let's Pray:
Heavenly Father, help me to never seek after a sign. Give me strength to believe in you, trust in you, and follow you closely. I know the signs will come. Let me always rely on your goodness and love even when times are dark. I know you will bring the answer I need, in your time. In Jesus' name, Amen!

100 Days With Jesus

Day 26
Matthew 17

CHOOSE YOUR BATTLES

"However, so that we do not offend them, go to the sea and throw in a hook, and take the first fish that comes up; and when you open its mouth, you will find a shekel. Take that and give it to them for you and Me."
- Matthew 17:27

In our scripture today, we are given a small but fascinating insight into the character and mission of Jesus. Some tax collectors had asked Peter whether or not Jesus paid the two-drachma tax. Peter said He did. Jesus then asks Peter who pays taxes, the king's sons or strangers. Peter says strangers. Jesus agrees and says that sons are exempt.

What is Jesus saying here with this small exchange? He is declaring His Sonship to Peter and to us. He is declaring that He is the Son who doesn't need to pay taxes. Son of whom? Not Joseph the carpenter. That son would need to pay every tax. No, He is declaring for all time that He is the Son of God. This obscure moment in His earthly teaching carries a profound truth.

But then He tells Peter to pay the tax. Why? He just said that He is exempt, so why pay? Why not fight that unrighteous tax? After all, people have been fighting about taxes for thousands of years and still do. If Jesus was a modern-day politician, He would have broadcast some negative ads about the current administration. And

A Journey Through The Gospels

Jesus could be very aggressive in His criticisms of the ruling classes. Why not here?

Jesus is wisely choosing His battles. This is such a small thing; it's not worth His time to fight about it. Jesus has a much bigger fish to fry: sin. He has a much more important goal: the lost sheep. He has a much bigger battle to win: the salvation of you and me.

What needless battles are we fighting? Some battles should be fought every day; others should be dropped immediately. Don't worry too much about having to be right. It's more important to be healed, and to have peace. Ask the Lord to show you the right battles.

Let's Pray:
Lord, show me where to fight and where to relent.
Show me how to achieve peace in the situations
I am facing. Help me to battle vigorously for the things
that really matter while also keeping a godly character
throughout the process. Thank you for the victory!
In Jesus' name, Amen!

100 Days With Jesus

Day 27
Matthew 18 — GREATNESS

> *At that time the disciples came to Jesus and said, "Who then is greatest in the kingdom of Heaven?"* - Matthew 18:1

Andrew and Philip were having an intense discussion. They looked at the twelve disciples and wondered who was the greatest. Andrew said, "It has to be Peter. After all he is the Rock, isn't he?" Philip responded, "I don't know. He's your brother and all, but he messes things up a lot. Foot-in-mouth problems, you know. What about James and John? They're supposed to be Sons of Thunder." Andrew responded, "They don't quite get Jesus' love for people. Remember that 'call-down-fire' fiasco? They've got to get their motivation right." Matthew, sitting nearby, decided to join in, "And their mother is always trying to get the best for them. I wish she would butt out." Then the three all sat alone with their thoughts for a while, pondering in their heart, "Maybe I could be the greatest. Someone has to lead, right?" After a few moments, Andrew broke the silence and said, "Maybe it's someone we don't even know yet. Let's ask Jesus."

We can imagine such discussions happening among the disciples. They were brought up under a system that prized grandeur. It put an emphasis on pomp and appearance. They had a king, Herod, that had a palace and lots of finery. They had a high priest and a priestly order that had a lot of outward show. Even the Romans,

A Journey Through The Gospels

whom they despised, had their shiny armor. To them, everything a leader was supposed to be included a display of outward strength and abundance. So, when they asked Jesus who was the greatest in the kingdom, they weren't expecting this answer:

And He called a child to Himself and set him before them, and said, "Truly I say to you, unless you are converted and become like children, you will not enter the kingdom of Heaven. Whoever then humbles himself as this child, he is the greatest in the kingdom of Heaven" (Matthew 18:2-4).

Jesus, as usual, is turning the discussion on its head. Do we realize by now that the kingdom of God is completely different than an earthly realm? The kingdom of Heaven is built upside down. Here is one of the clearest examples of that truth. Children lead nothing; they are not presidents or prime ministers or kings. They have the lowest positions of responsibility. So why are they the key to being great in God's kingdom?

Children are *dependent.* They realize their inabilities and rely on their parents to help them. We must realize our own need to depend on God. No one who clings to their independence can ever enter into the kingdom of Heaven. Only children get in.

Let's Pray:
God, I pray to have a child-like dependence on you. Help me to love like a child, laugh like a child, and lean on you like a child. Give me strength to serve your kingdom from the bottom up. In Jesus' name, Amen!

100 Days With Jesus

Day 28
Matthew 19   WHAT GOOD THING?

And someone came to Him and said, "Teacher, what good thing shall I do that I may obtain eternal life?" - Matthew 19:16

Jesus was out in the street doing what He always did: teaching, healing and interacting with the people. Jesus was, and is, an accessible Savior. A young man, a man of importance, approached Him. This guy was a real dandy. He had on the best clothes, Gucci robes perhaps. His hair was perfect, and he smelled like the most popular perfume. This rich, young ruler came up to Jesus and asked Him the question in our text today. He wanted to obtain eternal life.

What a great intro for a gospel presentation! This will be like shooting fish in a barrel for Jesus. Here is someone who will surely join up with his merry band of followers. But the Lord asks him some questions and then drops the bomb on him: *Jesus said to him, "If you wish to be complete, go and sell your possessions and give to the poor, and you will have treasure in heaven; and come, follow Me" (Matthew 19:21).*

I don't know about you, but I've never given these instructions to anyone. It's not in *The Four Spiritual Laws* or the *Steps to Peace with God* tracts. Billy Graham never gave an altar call at one of

A Journey Through The Gospels

his crusades where he said to come forward and receive Christ and, "Oh yeah, now sell your car and your house, and give the money to that homeless guy on Sixth Avenue, and you will be saved." No evangelist has this as part of their salvation message. But Jesus does for this guy. Why?

Jesus can see right through us. The rich young ruler was trusting in his ability to be good. He had kept all the commandments. He was confident in his abilities. Things had gone his way his whole life. Wasn't his position and wealth already a sign of his holiness? Nope. In fact, Jesus is about to blow the disciples' minds concerning wealth. But on the larger topic of salvation, Jesus knew that this man's riches would be a barrier to his total commitment to Him. And it was: *"But when the young man heard this statement, he went away grieving; for he was one who owned much property* (Matthew 19:22).

Following Jesus is never a part-time job. It's 100% commitment. Salvation is a free gift. We cannot buy it. But if we lose everything, we will find Him!

Let's Pray:
Lord Jesus, I want to be your follower with no strings attached. Help me to "sell off" anything that takes your place in my life. Let nothing hold me back from being your disciple! In Jesus' name, Amen!

100 Days With Jesus

Day 29
Matthew 20 — *GOD'S GENEROSITY*

So the last shall be first, and the first last. - Matthew 20:16

Jesus has just finished telling a story to the disciples. He tells of a landowner who needed workers in his field. He hired some in the early morning, agreeing to pay them one denarius. Then he hired some more at lunchtime, and then some in late afternoon. When the time came for them to collect their pay, they all got paid the same: one denarius. The men who had worked all day grumbled about this.

Let's put this in modern terms. You agree to paint someone's house for $15 an hour for ten hours. Not too bad. Hard work in the hot sun, but you'll have $150 at the end of the day. (No IRS in this story.) It's a big job though, and you're not going to get it done by yourself, so he hires a second guy right after lunch. Yay! You've got some help. You can give him the windows to paint! Finally, at 4:00 PM, the homeowner hires ten more guys. He really wants this house done today! It's kind of tricky, but once they all have brushes, the house is done by dinnertime.

Now it's time to get paid, and he starts with the last guys. To your surprise, he pays them each $150! Wow! You can't wait till he gets to you. You're going to get $1000, at least! But when your turn comes, you get the same $150. Now, for that which you were

A Journey Through The Gospels

happy to get at the start, you are now angry. This is unfair! I'm going to the National Labor Relations Board! I'll sue! We would all feel this way, but that is not the point of the story. Jesus is not teaching us a seminar on employee compensation. He is sharing with us something about the kingdom of God.

Many of us have served God for a long time. We have been through many "dangers, toils, and snares." It has been good to know the Lord, but it hasn't always been easy. The thing that has kept us faithful is knowing our eternal home was secure. But what about the late-comers? What about those who got saved late in life? Then they come to church and get honored. They share their testimony and everyone cheers. Then they are put in charge of the Sunday School. In five years, they are pastoring your church. How are we supposed to feel about that?

We are supposed to rejoice! Many will come late to the faith, but they will be just as saved as you and me. More importantly, we are to be the ones inviting them in. Jesus said we are to go into, *"the highways and the hedges and compel them to come in."* Seeing His stray sheep come into the sheepfold is what pleases the heart of the Savior.

Let's Pray:
Heavenly Father, let me always be about the work
of your kingdom. Let me have your heart for those outside.
Break my heart with the things that break your heart,
Lord. Let me see many come inside. In Jesus' name, Amen!

100 Days With Jesus

Day 30
Matthew 21

MAKING IT CLEAR

When He had entered Jerusalem, all the city was stirred, saying, "Who is this?" - Matthew 21:10

The people of Jerusalem were confused about Jesus. They were hearing Him say amazing things and watching Him perform incredible miracles. Their religious leaders said all kind of bad things about Him; fake, false prophet, deceiver, and more. But how could so many wonderful things come from a deceiver? Jerusalem was a conflicted place.

Matthew 21 gives us divinely inspired insight into who Jesus is. Let's look at what it reveals about this man.

He is the Lord.
"If anyone says anything to you, you shall say, 'The Lord has need of them,' and immediately he will send them" (Matthew 21:3).
Jesus is the Lord of Heaven and earth. Nothing is impossible for Him.

He is the King.
"Say to the daughter of Zion, 'Behold your King is coming to you, Gentle, and mounted on a donkey, even on a colt, the foal of a beast of burden'" (Matthew 21:5). Jesus is a humble King. He doesn't ride in a chariot; He doesn't ride on a white stallion; He rides on a borrowed donkey.

A Journey Through The Gospels

He is the Messiah.
The crowds going ahead of Him, and those who followed, were shouting, "Hosanna to the Son of David" (Matthew 21:9). "Son of David" is a messianic title. The people knew what they were saying. So did the Pharisees, and they didn't like it. By the way, "Hosanna" means "Save us!"

He is God.
"But when the chief priests and the scribes saw the wonderful things that He had done, and the children who were shouting in the temple, 'Hosanna to the Son of David,' they became indignant and said to Him, 'Do You hear what these children are saying?' And Jesus said to them, 'Yes; have you never read, 'Out of the mouth of infants and nursing babies You have prepared praise for Yourself?'" (Matthew 21:15-16).

This is the strongest declaration of all. The verse Jesus quotes is from the Old Testament, Psalm 8. It refers to God there, and it refers to God here. Remember, God alone is to receive worship. By accepting worship from the multitudes, Jesus is declaring Himself to be God in the flesh. We always need to remember who Jesus is. When we face our struggles today He is everything that we need!

Let's Pray:
*Lord, you are a mighty God and Lord. You are much
bigger than any giants that I will face today.
Let me always remember who you are!
In Jesus' name, Amen!*

100 Days With Jesus

Day 31
Matthew 22   REALITY VIEW

On that day some Sadducees (who say there is no resurrection) came to Jesus and questioned Him. - Matthew 22:23

The Pharisees and Sadducees were always trying to trap Jesus into saying something wrong and prove to everyone that He was not a real prophet. The Pharisees tried to capture Him in his theology. They never could, of course, so the Sadducees thought of a new tactic. They would catch Jesus in a riddle of logic, something that was unanswerable. The Sadducees were the intellectual smart alecks of first-century Jerusalem, and they were in rare form on this day.

They posed a question to Jesus to "prove" there is no afterlife, no resurrection of the dead. Here it is: *"There were seven brothers. The first one married a wife and then he died. In obedience to the law of Moses, the woman married the second brother, who also died. In fact, all seven brothers died (this family definitely needed to exercise more) and the wife had been married to all of them. Finally, she died. So, in the resurrection whose wife will she be?"*

"Gotcha, Jesus!" You can almost hear them chuckle to themselves. But Jesus was never out-witted or out-smarted. He knew what to say to them, *"You are mistaken, not understanding the Scriptures*

A Journey Through The Gospels

nor the power of God. For in the resurrection they neither marry nor are given in marriage but are like angels in heaven" (Matthew 22: 29b-30). Jesus shows them the error of their story, and in so doing, begins to detail the reality of the resurrection. On that topic He has another point to make. *"But regarding the resurrection of the dead, have you not read what was spoken to you by God: 'I am the God of Abraham, and the God of Isaac, and the God of Jacob'? He is not the God of the dead but of the living"* (Matthew 22: 31-32).

Jesus gives them a great answer. He has won the "debate," but He is not interested in that. What is He really after? Good theology? Yes, but so much more. He loves the Sadducees! He wants them to become followers, to be saved, to be filled with the Holy Spirit, to preach the true gospel to the ends of the earth. He wants them to experience the power of the Resurrection.

Modern Sadducees may come against you with their questions and comments. Don't be alarmed. Keep God's real purposes in mind. Ask God to help you see them as God sees them. Pray to feel His heart for them. Ask Him to help you keep the reality of the resurrection in view.

Let's Pray:
Heavenly Father, help me to see people as you see them. Let me experience your heart for them. If they cause me grief and trouble, Lord, let me never respond in the same manner. Open their hearts to see and accept your love today. In Jesus' name, Amen!

100 Days With Jesus

Day 32
Matthew 23

PRIDE AND PREJUDICE

Woe to you, scribes and Pharisees, hypocrites! - Matthew 23:23a

*R*abbi Daniel was hurrying along this morning. He wanted to see this prophet that he had heard so much about. A large crowd was gathering, including some of his rabbinical brethren. He was wearing his finest robes (what does one wear to hear a prophet anyway?) when he noticed the sign on Samuel's tailor shop. "Special Today! Tassels lengthened and phylacteries broadened! Stop in for our 2 for 1 sale!" "Hmmm," he thought to himself, "maybe I'll stop in after hearing Jesus today." He then went on his merry way.

Our dear rabbi had no idea what was in store for him as he walked into Jesus' sermon in Matthew 23. The Lord was about to launch into one His most pointed messages. He directs His opening comments against the hypocrisy of Jerusalem's religious leaders.

"Therefore, all that they tell you, do and observe, but do not do according to their deeds; for they say things and do not do them. They tie up heavy burdens and lay them on men's shoulders, but they themselves are unwilling to move them with so much as a finger. But they do all their deeds to be noticed by men; for they broaden their phylacteries and lengthen the tassels of their garments. They love the place of honor at banquets and the chief seats in the synagogues, and respectful greetings in the market places, and being called Rabbi by men" (Matthew 23:3-7).

A Journey Through The Gospels

Ouch! Jesus is holding nothing back; piercing the Pharisees' hypocrisy first, then going right after their spiritual pride.

Pride is a strange word. Taking pride in a job well done is a good thing. It is fine to be proud of your kids. However, spiritual pride is that which holds ourselves above others. There is no redeeming quality in this type of pride; in fact, it can keep us from knowing God. C.S. Lewis made the powerful observation: "As long as you are proud you cannot know God." We also remember Jesus' parable about the two men who went to the temple. The Pharisee had spiritual pride, the tax collector was humble before God. The tax collector went home forgiven and in right standing with God. The Pharisee did not.

Jesus then strikes on one of his favorite themes. *"But the greatest among you shall be your servant. Whoever exalts himself shall be humbled; and whoever humbles himself shall be exalted"* (Matthew 23:11-12). Jesus is getting at the heart of the matter, as He always does. He reminds us again and again that His kingdom has a different agenda. The first shall be last. The way down is the way up. Servanthood is greatness. I doubt that Samuel's tailor shop had much business that day!

Let's Pray:

Father, let me be aware of every ounce of spiritual pride in my own life. Make me realize that you alone are the source of anything good that is in me. Let me follow the way of Jesus in my relationship to you and to the outside world. Let me always walk in humility. In Jesus' name, Amen!

100 Days With Jesus

Day 33
Matthew 24   **TEMPORARY TEMPLES**

> *Jesus came out from the temple and was going away when His disciples came up to point out the temple buildings to Him. And He said to them, "Do you not see all these things? Truly I say to you, not one stone here will be left upon another, which will not be torn down."* - Matthew 24:1-2

About ten years ago, my father-in-law was honored for his service in the Second World War. His former army division had all gathered together in Washington, DC for a very special banquet, and Jean and I, and our son Andrew, attended the festivities. Most of the former soldiers were in their mid-to-late 80's, and it was one of the last gatherings for that honored group. It was a great event.

There was some down time, so my family went out to walk around the area. We were staying about two blocks from the White House, so we headed there. As we stood in front of the presidential mansion, I was struck by the large number of foreign tourists there to take pictures. We continued to walk through that part of our capital city, and I was filled with pride as I observed the awesome surroundings. If you've ever been to DC, you know what I'm talking about. Whether you're at the Capitol, the Lincoln Memorial or the Library of Congress, the buildings are solid, majestic, and beautiful. They give you a sense of history and permanence.

They are, however, temporary. No matter how majestic, how well built, and how important, there will ultimately come a day when

A Journey Through The Gospels

they will be gone. Jesus' disciples felt that the temple was a permanent structure. Far more than a seat of political power, the temple was the place where God's manifest presence dwelt. Surely Jesus would be impressed with those buildings, too. I mean, they were ordained by God Himself.

In our text today, Jesus uses this opportunity to say that the temple will be destroyed. This is inconceivable and shocking to the disciples. Jesus' prophecy comes true in 70 AD when the temple was destroyed by the Romans. So, what was Jesus trying to teach us? He went on to launch into a teaching about the end times, but I think His quick dismissal of the temple says something else to us. It says the temple is no longer needed.

With the coming of the Messiah, the temple had served its purpose. Jesus said that something greater than the temple is here (Matthew 12:6). Now, you have Christ in you, the hope of glory (Colossians 1:27). You ARE the temple of the Holy Spirit (1 Corinthians 3:16). You carry the life of God with you wherever you go. Let us be faithful witnesses to that which is really important, Christ Himself!

Let's Pray:
God, give me an eternal perspective on all I see.
Remind me Lord, that we work for fruit that will
last forever. It is the treasure that moths will not eat
nor rust destroy. Help me to work for the things
of heavenly value and true permanence.
In Jesus' name, Amen!

100 Days With Jesus

Day 34
Matthew 25

FIRST HAND SPIRITUALITY

But at midnight there was a shout, "Behold, the bridegroom! Come out to meet him." - Matthew 25:6

She ran through the streets and down an alleyway. "I must get him out of bed," she said in self-encouraging tones. Frantically, she tried to remember where the oil dealer lived. Finally, she found his home and woke him up, pleading, "Please, please please ... I need this oil! The bridegroom is here." "I told you to get some yesterday, Number 6," the shopkeeper angrily replied. He was a good man, however, and he relented. He opened the shop door with a creak, found the lamp oil, and filled her small lamp. "Hurry now," he said, "perhaps there is still time." Virgin Number 6 flew out the door and back to the waiting area, hoping that she was not too late.

In the previous chapter, Jesus had been warning His disciples to be ready for His coming. With the hindsight of 2,000 years, we understand that He is speaking of His second coming. I doubt the disciples really understood what He meant. Jesus continues in Matthew 25 on the same subject with the parable of the Ten Virgins. Both of these passages have the same message: *"Be on alert! You don't know when Christ will return, so do the things you should be doing."*

A Journey Through The Gospels

The parable of the Ten Virgins has the added message of proper preparation for the long haul. The Christian life is a marathon, not a sprint. I've known new Christians who started out like they were going to win the gold medal in the Christian hundred-yard dash. Sadly, many of them burned out quickly. But there is another part of this parable that speaks to me.

The foolish virgins tried to borrow some oil off the wise virgins. *"No," they replied, "there may not be enough for both us and you. Instead, go to those who sell oil and buy some for yourselves"* (Matthew 25:9, NIV). The point is this: You cannot borrow someone else's spirituality! Your relationship with the Lord must be yours, not your parents, not your spouse's, not your pastor's. You must know God for yourself. If you do, you will be ready when the bridegroom comes.

───────────

As she breathlessly ran down the street, Virgin Number 6 heard a trumpet. She dropped to her knees and wept.

Let's Pray:
Lord, I want to be ready for your coming.
Let my lamp always be full of the oil of the Holy Spirit.
Let my relationship to you be close,
so close that I rejoice at your coming.
In Jesus' name I pray, Amen!

100 Days With Jesus

Day 35
Matthew 26

HOW GREAT A LOVE

Going a little farther, He fell with His face to the ground and prayed, "My Father, if it is possible, may this cup be taken from Me. Yet not as I will, but as You will." - Matthew 26:39 (NIV)

Jesus is facing the greatest challenge of His life. He knows what He is about to go through, and He isn't looking forward to it. When Jesus called out to God in the Garden of Gethsemane for this cup to pass from Him, for what was He praying? Was He feeling fear of the crucifixion and asking to be freed from that? Probably so, but it goes deeper than that. He was facing a great agony. An agony like no one has known before or since. There are at least three types of agony He faces in our chapter today.

The agony of Betrayal. Jesus celebrates the last supper with His friends, including His friend, Judas. For three and a half years they have traveled everywhere together, ate together, slept in close quarters and shared the scriptures together. Now, He was about to leave them. One of those closest to Him was a devil. Judas heard all of the teachings, saw all of the miracles, saw the heart of God in Jesus, and still betrayed Him for thirty silver pieces.

The agony of Separation. Since eternity past, the Father and Son had enjoyed close fellowship with one another. The closest fellowship possible. Even when Jesus was here on earth, He had a close relationship with His Heavenly Father. That was all about

A Journey Through The Gospels

to change. He was facing a separation like none have ever gone through. He was about to say, *"My God, My God, why have You forsaken Me?"* The agony of not seeing the face of God must have been the greatest pain to bear.

The agony of Bearing our Sin. Jesus was about to take all the sin of the world upon Himself. Every form of greed, hate, envy, lust, and injustice that was ever done was about to be laid on His shoulders. Every sin I've committed and you've committed were in that mix, too. Even for the Son of God, this must have been a fearful prospect.

Jesus faces all this agony and more to lay His life down for you and me. He laid his life down for Peter, who was about to deny Him. He was about to die for Billy Graham, Mother Teresa, Abraham Lincoln, Saint Francis, and every good person you've ever known. He was also about to die for every evil person, too. Everyone's sin was wrapped up in His sacrifice. He came to save the whole world.

Let's Pray:
Jesus, your example of love is great.
I can't love people like that in my own strength.
Give me your love today for everyone I meet,
even those who don't love me.
In your name, Amen!

100 Days With Jesus

Day 36
Matthew 27   ## HE CAME FOR US

> *"Which of the two do you want me to release to you?" asked the governor. "Barabbas," they answered. "What shall I do, then, with Jesus who is called the Messiah?" Pilate asked. They all answered, "Crucify him!" "Why? What crime has he committed?" asked Pilate. But they shouted all the louder, "Crucify him!"* - Matthew 27:21-23 (NIV)

Long ago, in the depths of eternity past, it was decided that God the Son would come to earth and die a cruel death on a cross. He would do this to save the race of mankind. Many of the angels must have wondered at the compassion and love of God that He would allow His Son to die for others. These beings, mankind, that were not created yet, must have been very worthy of God's love for Him to sacrifice so much for them. The angels waited patiently for the creation to be completed and the breath of life to be put into Adam.

It's hard for us to understand this scenario. How could it be determined that Jesus would die beforehand? And yet the scriptures declare it. Peter preaches it in his first sermon: *"This Man, delivered over by the predetermined plan and foreknowledge of God, you nailed to a cross by the hands of godless men and put Him to death"* (Acts 2:23). In Revelation 13:8, the Bible declares that Jesus is: *the Lamb slain from the foundation of the world.* So God, who knew that men would fall, had a grand plan to save mankind.

A Journey Through The Gospels

But what about the idea that mankind was so great a creation that they were worthy of God's sacrifice? I'm afraid we fall short on that count, don't we? All of us do. This is brutally illustrated in our passage today. Jesus stood before the crowd, with nothing but overwhelming love in His heart for each person. And those same people asked for a murderer to be released instead of the Savior. Then they yelled for Pilate to put Him to death on a cross. Jesus was rejected by the very ones for which He came to die.

Thankfully, His love is everlasting. We all have rejected Jesus in one way or another. You and I deserved the cross. Our sins could have put us there, but they didn't. His love compelled Him to go. He went for us. *"See what great love the Father has lavished on us, that we should be called children of God! And that is what we are"* (1 John 3:1 NIV)!

Let's Pray:
Lord Jesus, I am overwhelmed by your love
that saved me and keeps me close to you.
Let me never neglect your love.
Draw me close today, Lord.
I love you! In your name, Amen!

100 Days With Jesus

Day 37
Matthew 28:1-15　　　　　　　　　　THE MESSAGE

And behold, a severe earthquake had occurred, for an angel of the Lord descended from Heaven and came and rolled away the stone and sat upon it. - Matthew 28:2

As she ran down the road, Mary reeled at the thought of what she had just seen. How can it be true? But it was true! She had seen Him, touched Him, He spoke to her! She thought of the despair of the last three days: His mock trial before the Jews, His horrible crucifixion at the hands of the Romans, His death and burial. All hope had been lost. She, along with His other disciples, had thought that He would take over, but then He was gone. A profound sadness had settled on the whole group, but especially on Peter. He was a mess. They all were.

But now, somehow, some way, He was alive! He told her to tell His disciples the news. She couldn't wait. Now the upper room where they were hiding was in view. She ran up the steps in a bound and knocked at the door. "Open up! I have the greatest news!" "What is it?" they said, still in a sullen mood. Mary then said the most powerful words she had ever spoken, "I have seen the Lord!"

Have you ever met someone on the bus, or at a party, or somewhere else, and felt an urge to speak to them about Jesus? I'm sure that

A Journey Through The Gospels

you have. The Holy Spirit that dwells inside of you and all believers is an evangelistic Spirit. He has as His greatest desire to bring others to a knowledge of God. The way He primarily does this is to work on a person's heart through the words that we speak to them.

So, what would you say to that person on the bus? Well, you could tell them about your church, or a book you are reading, or your favorite preacher. You could tell them about truths of the Bible. You could tell them the plan of salvation. These are all good things. But don't forget to tell them what Mary told the disciples. *"I have seen the Lord."*

Never underestimate your personal experience with the Lord. You KNOW God. That is a powerful statement and something that the other person does not have. A pastor of mine is fond of saying that a person with an experience is never at the mercy of a person with a theory. You, my Christian bus-riding friend, have seen the Lord!

Let's Pray:
Lord Jesus, thank you that I know you.
Thank you for drawing me into a relationship with you.
Help me to carry the same message to others
that Mary carried to the disciples.
In your name, Amen!

100 Days With Jesus

Day 38
Matthew 28:16-20 — **THE GREAT WHAT?**

"Go therefore and make disciples of all the nations, baptizing them in the name of the Father and the Son and the Holy Spirit, teaching them to observe all that I commanded you; and lo, I am with you always, even to the end of the age." - Matthew 28:19-20

We can't leave Matthew without considering the last two verses. Jesus gives His final command to his disciples. They are to take the message of His love and salvation to the entire world. These men and women had been with Jesus and seen His love, glory, miracles and most of all, His resurrection from the dead. They were in a unique position to carry out this command.

This final command is now referred to as *The Great Commission*. The disciples were given this joyous task and, not only them, but all believers have been commissioned to share the gospel with the world. So, let's look a little closer at what we have been asked to do.

Go – this small beginning word has incredible implications. We are not told to stay and preach the gospel. We are to GO somewhere. "Go" inherently means to change your location. We all know that if we go to the store, or to the ballgame, or on vacation, that we are leaving our home and going somewhere else. Surprisingly, many Christians do not realize that to fulfill the Great Commission we must GO somewhere. It could be across the street or downtown, but it might mean so much more. That brings us to the next word.

A Journey Through The Gospels

Nations – Billy Graham said, "Jesus belongs to all people, He belongs to the whole world." So, in order to fulfill the Great Commission, we are going to have to be willing to cross national boundaries. The gospel has no borders.

Baptizing and Teaching – This is salvation and discipleship. This is our message. We proclaim the salvation found in Christ and then continue to teach in order that we may, as Paul said, "present every man complete in Christ."

I think all of us know about the Great Commission. We know that the church has a call to reach the world. However, sometimes we fail to connect the dots to ourselves. The Great Commission is not just for preachers. It is not the domain of professionals. You and I can reach the world for Christ, too. All we need to do is ***Go!***

Let's Pray:
Lord, give me an opportunity to reach a person for you today.
Show me where I should go and to whom I should speak.
Help me to care about a world that you love!
In Jesus' name, Amen!

100 Days With Jesus

Day 39
Mark 1 INSTANT

Immediately He called them; and they left their father Zebedee in the boat with the hired servants, and went away to follow Him. - Mark 1:20

Zebedee looked up with calm surprise as he saw James and John get out of the boat. The hired men were shocked. Jared, one of the longest serving men, said to Zebedee, "Where are they going? Why have they left? Who is that man?" Zebedee had no answers, but something inside of him knew that his sons were doing right. There was a peaceful assurance in his heart that the man was a prophet sent by God for His people, Israel. If that was the case, then Zebedee would gladly release his sons to follow. What had He said? "I will make you fishers of men." What a strange turn of a phrase! Zebedee pondered that a long time in his heart.

Have you ever marveled at how quickly James and John followed the Savior's call? I mean, Jesus just said one quick sentence and they left their father, their business, and their future there on the dock. They left every bit of security and everything familiar to them to take a step in Jesus' direction. And for what? What was the appeal of this prophet?

Maybe they had heard of Him. Perhaps they had heard one of His

A Journey Through The Gospels

sermons. Did the promise of being "fishers of men" intrigue them? I'm sure all of this is true, but there is more to it than that. James and John must have seen the hope of a better future for their family and for their nation. They saw in Jesus one who could save them. But I think there was even a stronger draw.

They saw Jesus! They saw the Son of God. They saw God incarnate, in the flesh. They saw the long-promised Messiah, the One who would save God's people from their sins. This was more than a man … He was a man they could leave all to follow.

What is Jesus' call to you today? What does He ask you to leave, to lay down or to sacrifice? No matter how great the cost to follow Christ, it will be worth it. He will make you a fisher of men.

Let's Pray:
Jesus help me to clearly see and hear your call
to me today. More than that, give me the commitment
to leave all to follow you. I want to be close
to you today and always.
In your name I pray, Amen!

100 Days With Jesus

Day 40
Mark 2

DESPERATE FRIENDSHIP

Being unable to get to Him because of the crowd, they removed the roof above Him; and when they had dug an opening, they let down the pallet on which the paralytic was lying. - Mark 2:4

I sat there transfixed as Jesus spoke. Here I was, a Pharisee, a teacher of the Law, one who should know God better than others, but Jesus' teaching had much more authority than mine. He spoke with an ease, a knowledge of God of which He was rock-sure. More than that, Jesus spoke of a God He knew! Not knowledge about God, but relationship with Him. I wanted more of this God. Suddenly, there was noise on the roof and sunlight streamed in! What could this be?

———

Our Pharisee above just wanted to learn. He wanted to sit at the feet of the great Teacher and be taught. But Jesus was about to do much more. Jesus came to set people free. He is just beginning His ministry, and the gospel writer Mark wastes no time in getting right into the meat, recording the passage above. Jesus came not just to teach, but to seek and to save that which was lost.

This scenario in Mark 2 doesn't happen without the love of the paralytic's friends. They have seen their friend suffering for years, and they see this holy man of God is doing miracles. It's a great idea to take their friend to Jesus, but oh, it's too crowded! What

A Journey Through The Gospels

should we do? Go home? No, that is not an option. They love their friend too much to let that happen. They are desperate for their friend to be healed. So, their love finds another way.

The paralytic is hopeful of healing, but Jesus gives him something else. I can see Jesus is blessed and maybe slightly amused at the delivery of this man to Him. He smiles and says, "Your sins are forgiven." The man who wanted healing is getting salvation. And he gets healing, also. The gathered crowd gets something, too. They see that this is more than a prophet who is speaking. He has authority to forgive sins. They left, glorifying God for what they had seen.

Friendship brings healing. Who do you know who needs healing? Who do you know who needs to meet the Savior? It is time to climb on the roof for them.

Let's Pray:
God, I thank you for the friends and loved ones
you have used to bless me.
Please help me to be that friend who blesses others.
Help me to bring them to you, whatever it takes.
In Jesus' name, Amen!

100 Days With Jesus

Day 41
Mark 3 ——— **TRUE RELIGION**

And He said to them, "Is it lawful to do good or to do harm on the Sabbath, to save a life or to kill?" But they kept silent. - Mark 3:4

Have you ever tried to tell someone about Jesus, and they say something like, "I'm not religious." This is supposed to end the discussion. They deem you or me as a "religious person," and they don't want any part of that. What they fail to realize is we want no part of that type of religion either.

The Pharisees were a religious bunch. They kept all of God's laws, or at least they thought they did. They kept the outward ones for sure. Someone could look at one of them and see a holy man. However, what was going on inside of them was far from a holy picture. Jesus addressed this when He spoke to them later and said, *"Woe to you, scribes and Pharisees, hypocrites! For you are like whitewashed tombs, which outwardly appear beautiful, but within are full of dead people's bones and all uncleanness"* (Matthew 23:27, ESV).

We can learn a lot from the Pharisees. We can learn how not to be! It's obvious that we don't want to be outwardly spiritual and inwardly sinful. We want to let God clean the inside of our heart. Then the outside will take care of itself.

A Journey Through The Gospels

There is another lesson, though, that speaks more directly in this passage. We want to be people who, unlike the Pharisees, have the heart of God for others. Jesus asks them a very simple question in our lead scripture today, *"Is it lawful… ?"* The heart of God is to do good, to heal even on, especially on, the Sabbath.

Look at these guys! They want to see if Jesus will heal on the Sabbath, and when He does, do they change their tune and say, "Well, this man must really be from God." Nope. They double down on their hypocrisy and begin to plot how to destroy Him! But God is at work. A man has been made whole, and though it is not recorded in scripture, we can be reasonably sure that he goes on to glorify God. Yet the ones who should be glorifying God are His enemies.

We need to have the heart of God for others — the hurting and the destitute. The challenge for us is not to condemn the Pharisees, but rather, to be like Christ.

Let's Pray:
Heavenly Father, please give me your heart
of compassion for all people everywhere.
Give me your heart for one person today. Use me
to heal their brokenness through your power.
In Jesus' name, Amen!

100 Days With Jesus

Day 42
Mark 4 STORM RISING

> *And a great windstorm arose, and the waves beat into the boat, so that it was already filling. But He was in the stern, asleep on a pillow. And they awoke Him and said to Him, "Teacher, do You not care that we are perishing?"*
> - Mark 4:37-38 (NKJV)

I stood on the bridge of the mercy ship, Anastasis, looking at the prow far below. A question was asked about sailing in bad weather. Our tour guide said that under normal sea conditions, the prow of the ship will continuously go down under the water and come back up as they sail across the ocean. To me, an inexperienced traveler on the sea, this seemed inconceivable. Then the guide said that there are times, in rough weather, that the prow never comes out of the water! It just rocks up and down, but the waves are too high for the prow to break through. Still the ship sails on. (I made a mental note to never volunteer for ship ministry!)

In our scripture today, the disciples were quite afraid. These were largely experienced seamen, but the force of the gale was enough to frighten even them. They knew that Jesus could rescue them, but He was asleep in the boat. The enemy used this situation to bring doubt into their minds, doubt about the character of God. They roused Jesus and asked Him why He didn't care that they were perishing. Doesn't this sound like our thoughts when we are going through a hard time? We wonder why Jesus didn't prevent

A Journey Through The Gospels

it from happening? We wonder where our abundant life is. And we wonder if He even cares.

Of course, Jesus did care. He got up and rebuked the wind and the sea became still. It was a great testimony to the divine nature of Christ. Jesus used this as a teachable moment for the disciples. Sounding a little groggy, I suspect, Jesus asked them why they had no faith.

Faith is made for times like these. When the seas are calm and a gentle breeze is blowing, it is easy to have faith in God. When the winds are howling and the ship is going under, we need our faith. This is the key: Faith is for the hard times. That is when we must trust God, trust in His love, and trust in His character. He will never leave us nor forsake us.

Let's Pray:
God give me the faith to believe you will calm the storm I am going through. Storms come in life but you are always in the boat with us.
I believe in you.
In Jesus' mighty name, Amen!

100 Days With Jesus

Day 43
Mark 5

TOO LATE?

> *While He was still speaking, some came from the ruler of the synagogue's house who said, "Your daughter is dead. Why trouble the Teacher any further?"*
> - Mark 5:35 (NKJV)

Jairus hustled his way through the crowded side street. Suddenly he burst out onto the main avenue, knocking over a shelf of vegetables. He didn't care. He needed to get to Jesus! People were everywhere. He pushed his way through the throngs and asked Jesus to come, and He said He would! They started to make their way to Jairus' home. If only they weren't too late! Suddenly, Jesus stopped, and Jairus thought his world would end.

Jairus was doing everything he could to save his daughter. He was an important man and he knew how to get things done, but here was something that he couldn't control. His daughter had to be saved by One who was greater than himself. She needed a miracle, and Jairus knew Jesus was a miracle worker. But seemingly, her miracle had been set aside for someone else.

There is an old question that skeptics like to ask, "How can God hear the prayers of everyone at the same time?" Sometimes I've even heard Christians say, "How can God care about my needs when He is so busy with the big problems in the world?" What

A Journey Through The Gospels

escapes their notice is that God is not limited by time. And He certainly doesn't work on our timetable.

Jairus was surely discouraged by the news that his daughter had died. His servants in our scripture today gave a true report, from an earthly point of view. They thought Jairus needed comfort, but he really needed to trust in the faithfulness of God. But Jesus, overhearing what was being spoken, said to the synagogue official, *"Do not be afraid any longer, only believe"* (Mark 5:36).

Does God seem to be lagging in His answer to your prayers? Is He too late? Trust in the Lord of Time. He is never late, as Jairus was about to find out. Jairus could not contain the tears as his daughter rose from the bed. The room was filled with the presence of God! He now knew this man Jesus was more than a prophet.

Let's Pray:
Lord, I have prayed long, and I haven't seen
the answer you promised. But I will continue
to trust you Lord. Give me faith like Jairus',
so that I will trust you even in the darkest hours.
In Jesus' name, Amen!

100 Days With Jesus

Day 44
Mark 6   ## COME AWAY

> And He said to them, "Come away by yourselves to a secluded place and rest a while." (For there were many people coming and going, and they did not even have time to eat.) They went away in the boat to a secluded place by themselves. - Mark 6:31-32

It was quitting time and everyone was heading home, walking past my desk in the distribution department. I had a lot more to do and realized that I wouldn't be following them for a while. I didn't mind so much. I was new to the company and was on a steep learning curve. I was putting my full-force into my job and needed to put in the extra time. My co-workers had noticed my efforts, as I had just won employee of the quarter. Things were going well. Still, I wasn't heading home.

Just then Larry, the vice-president of the company, walked by on his way out the door. He looked at me and said, "Remember to keep these things in balance." I got the message. I wrapped up quickly and headed home.

Mark 6 is just chock-full of activity. The disciples had just been sent out by Jesus to preach the gospel, cast out demons, and heal the sick. Soon Jesus was to feed the five thousand. More fruitful ministry and big challenges were on the way. As the disciples finished sharing the happy results of their mission trip, Jesus says an interesting thing, "Come away."

A Journey Through The Gospels

Rest is an essential part of our Christian lives. Everyone says they agree with that, but it is so easy to forget. God created us to need rest. We need sleep every night. We have to stop a few times each day to eat. He commanded Israel to take a day off each week. He gave them feasts. They had to leave their fields fallow once every seven years. Jesus himself often got away alone and, get this, He even took naps! (Remember what He was doing in the boat?)

Are we getting the picture? God delights in our rest and relaxation. Take time with God, with your family, and by yourself. Tomorrow will take care of itself.

Let's Pray:
Jesus, help me to follow your example
and take time for rejuvenation.
Let me take time for my family.
Let me take time to restore my soul.
In your name, Amen!

100 Days With Jesus

Day 45
Mark 7 LIKE A FIDDLER ON THE ROOF

"Neglecting the commandment of God, you hold to the tradition of men." - Mark 7:8

The classic motion picture musical, *Fiddler on The Roof*, is one of my and Jean's favorites. As you probably know, it follows the story of Tevye, a poor middle-aged Jewish dairy farmer in Russia, whose three teenage daughters are looking for love in all the wrong places. Well, at least wrong to Tevye. He states his case to each of them, saying that they need to follow tradition. He tells them, *"Without our traditions, our lives would be as shaky as... as... as a fiddler on the roof!"*

Tradition can indeed be a wonderful thing. Family and church traditions can connect us back to previous generations. They can remind us of the faithfulness of God in traditional ceremonies such as the Seder meal. However, Jesus has some harsh words about tradition in Mark 7.

The Pharisees were using tradition to control and bind people. Where God wanted freedom, they put man's traditions. Where God wanted a new move of the Spirit, they wanted to stay where they were. Listen to what Jesus says:

A Journey Through The Gospels

And He said to them, "Rightly did Isaiah prophesy of you hypocrites, as it is written: This people honors Me with their lips, But their heart is far away from Me. But in vain do they worship Me, teaching as doctrines the precepts of men.' Neglecting the commandment of God, you hold to the tradition of men." He was also saying to them, *"You are experts at setting aside the commandment of God in order to keep your tradition"* (Mark 6:6-9).

There is a lot we could discuss here, but the most important thing is to realize when God wants to do a new thing we must dispose of the traditions of men. Certainly, we must get rid of traditions that trap us in bondage. But even traditions that started out good must be set aside for the move of God to continue. The most chilling result of tradition's hold on the Pharisees was that it prevented them from recognizing their Messiah when He was standing right in front of them.

What tradition is holding us back from fully following God? Is there something old stopping the move of the new into your life? Is the old thing truly from God? Is it for now? If so, then hang on to it. If not, let it go!

Let's Pray:
God, I ask that you help me to follow your leading. Let me set aside anything from the past that is merely the tradition of men. Help me to be sensitive to you. In Jesus' name, Amen!

100 Days With Jesus

Day 46
Mark 8   *GOD'S INTERESTS*

And He began to teach them that the Son of Man must suffer many things and be rejected by the elders and the chief priests and the scribes, and be killed, and after three days rise again. - Mark 8:31

*P*eter could hardly believe what he was hearing. Jesus had just confirmed that He was the Messiah! Peter's heart leapt at the thought of Jesus and His coming kingdom! But wait, what was this? Jesus was saying that He was going to die. No, this can't be right! Peter was frustrated and confused. He began to get angry. No, Jesus! This isn't the way we thought it was going to go. Peter took Jesus aside to rebuke him. That didn't go very well.

No, it didn't go very well at all for Peter. Look at verse 33: *But turning around and seeing His disciples, He rebuked Peter and said, "Get behind Me, Satan; for you are not setting your mind on God's interests, but man's."* I don't know about you, but I really wouldn't like to be called Satan by Jesus. This is the sternest rebuke that Jesus ever brought against one of His disciples. What did Peter do that deserved such a reprimand? He set his mind on man's interests.

Jesus had just revealed and confirmed who He really was: the Christ, the Anointed One, the long-promised Messiah, the Son of the Living God. He is also coming very close to the time when He

A Journey Through The Gospels

will fulfill His mission. He is going to, *"Give His life as a ransom for many."* This is no time for Peter to confuse things.

Today, some liberal theologians will try to say that Jesus was merely a great teacher. They will say that there is much we can learn from Him, but that is all. Jesus would say that this is a message from Satan. Most of us realize that the full ministry of Christ was not merely teaching. However, even among Christians, there can be a tendency to place the focus on man's interests.

If we focus only on what being a Christian can do for me, on our fulfillment and our blessings, we rob the Son of God of His preeminent and glorious place. Following Christ will result in purpose and blessing. It will result in peace. But we must keep Him in first place in our lives. He must increase; we must decrease.

Let's Pray:
Jesus, you are indeed the Holy One.
Let me always keep my mind on God's purposes.
When times are good, I want all the glory to be yours.
When times are tough,
still I will praise you. You are the Lord.
In your name I pray, Amen!

100 Days With Jesus

Day 47
Mark 9

WHAT THEN?

As they were coming down from the mountain, He gave them orders not to relate to anyone what they had seen, until the Son of Man rose from the dead. They seized upon that statement, discussing with one another what rising from the dead meant. - Mark 9:9-10

The three were hiking down the Mount of Transfiguration still stunned. Peter, as usual, was the first one to speak up. "What did we just see?" he asked. James said, "You said it yourself when He asked you. Jesus isn't just a prophet; He is the Messiah. He is even the Son of God." John chimed in, "What did Jesus mean when He said that He would "rise from the dead"? Is He telling us another parable? He is the Son of God, how could He die?" The three walked a bit further in silence, pondering in their hearts what Jesus' words really meant. Peter, still stinging a bit from last week's rebuke by Jesus (*"Get behind me, Satan."*), felt he knew the answer. "It isn't a parable. Jesus is going to die. This is how He will finally defeat death by rising again!" Taking that in for a moment, John said, "What then?"

What then, indeed? The disciples were slowly beginning to realize the enormity of Jesus' mission. Like the sun coming up after a dark night, understanding was beginning to dawn on them. At first, they followed a prophet, then a leader, then a deliverer, then a

A Journey Through The Gospels

messiah, and finally the Son of God. His full mission, and theirs, wouldn't be fully revealed until after the resurrection. Then they would know what He meant by "rise from the dead."

They had left all to follow Christ. They did it without this full understanding they were now beginning to get. Why did they follow Him? Probably because they saw grace and truth in Jesus. They saw that here was a Man who could show them the Father. Philip even asked him, *"Lord show us the Father and it will be enough." Jesus said, "Anyone who has seen Me has seen the Father"* (John 14). That must have made their hair stand on end! But slowly they found out who Jesus really was.

How about you and me? We know from the scriptures that Jesus is the Lord, Savior, and God incarnate, but do we live like we know that? What would our lives look like if we really did? Peter, James, and John were fishermen, but once they caught sight of the Transfiguration, once they met the resurrected Christ, they were never the same again. What then? Then the world was never the same again.

Let's Pray:
Lord Jesus, please let me catch a glimpse of your glory. Let me be transformed by it. Then send me out with your message of salvation. Help me to transform my part of the world. In your precious name and for your glory, Amen!

100 Days With Jesus

Day 48
Mark 10 LITTLE ONES

And He took them in His arms and began blessing them, laying His hands on them. - Mark 10:16

Anger welled up inside of Maria. It wasn't the emotion with which she had started the day. She heard Jesus would be in town. She was thrilled with this new prophet, or maybe, One who was more than a prophet. She had heard of healings and miracles taking place through this man. Did He really raise someone from the dead? She didn't really need any miracle but she knew that her son, Jeremiah, wanted to see Him. They joyfully walked toward the meeting place. Suddenly, three big disciples were blocking their path. They told them not to bother Jesus. Maria wanted to shout, but just then Jesus motioned to them.

When we come to new life in Jesus Christ we become a new creature. Old things are passing away. We begin to live a new way, speak a new way, give a new way, and serve a new way. Some things take a little longer for us to learn, though. One of these is child-likeness.

Our scripture today illustrates one of the great mysteries of the kingdom of God. To be saved, we must become like children. The

A Journey Through The Gospels

disciples didn't want to be bothered with the children. Children don't behave. They are loud and messy. Jesus had important stuff to say and important things to do. The disciples mustn't let all that great ministry be interrupted by children.

Ah…how different the kingdom of God is. *"Permit the children to come to Me; do not hinder them; for the kingdom of God belongs to such as these. Truly I say to you, whoever does not receive the kingdom of God like a child will not enter it at all"* (Mark 10:14b-15). Jesus smiled at the boy closest to him. He began to lay hands on him and all the others as they came near, laughing for joy.

All our important things pale next to a child-like desire to be with Jesus. These children had that. Do we?

Let's Pray:
Jesus, how much I say I want to be with you.
Please let me not just pay lip service to my
relationship with you. Help me to realize that my joy
will always be found at the same place:
in your presence. Let me stay close to you today.
In your name, Amen!

100 Days With Jesus

Day 49
Mark 11

PASSION OF THE CHRIST

And He began to teach and say to them, "Is it not written, 'My house shall be called a house of prayer for all the nations'? But you have made it a robbers' den." - Mark 11:17

Amaziah began to set up his small table. "I expect it to be a good day today! The morning is fine and the people are lined up outside the temple." He was speaking with the vendor next to him, his friend Zachariah, who was also setting up. "I'm concerned, though," said Zach. "That Prophet Jesus, the Nazarene, has been seen in the city again. He's a troublemaker. I don't know what He'll do next. The priests are even confused by Him." "Well, if He truly is a prophet, then He'll come to the temple and offer sacrifices," said Amaziah. "That sounds like good business to me!" Looking up, both men saw a figure moving toward them at a quick pace. Zachariah snapped, "Head's up! I think that's Him coming now!" Amaziah chuckled, "Maybe He'll bless our offerings. More good business!"

The two friends in our scenario above were about to get the shock of their lives. Instead of coming with a blessing, Jesus was coming with a whip. We all know Jesus as the Good Shepherd who lays down His life for His sheep. We know Him as the one who came because of God's great love. We know Him as the one who gives

A Journey Through The Gospels

us rest for our souls. Here, Jesus is coming differently; He is coming in anger and judgement. Jesus never sinned. Everything that He did was completely holy and righteous, including casting out the money changers from the temple. So, we must wrestle with why this was right for Jesus to do.

Consider this: Jesus is actually acting in great compassion by turning over the tables. He sees the place His Father created to be a place of atonement and worship, had become a den of robbery. The sellers were cheating the people, not only of money, but also cheating them from complete access to God. The priests had put a roadblock in front of those seeking the Lord. Jesus is never going to take that idly.

Jesus lets his passion show and so should we. Do you have a passion? Is it from God? Is it in line with God's Word? Then follow it to the fullest, always keeping God's perspective in view. Let the passion of Jesus consume you!

Let's Pray:
Heavenly Father, just like Jesus,
let zeal for your house consume me!
In His name I pray, Amen!

100 Days With Jesus

Day 50
Mark 12   *THE LIVING GOD*

Jesus said to them, "Is this not the reason you are mistaken, that you do not understand the Scriptures or the power of God?" - Mark 12:24

Jimmy was dreading his sixth period class. Here he was, only in seventh grade, and he didn't think that he should have to face this. He just knew that Mr. Jurzack would challenge his faith in God in some way. Sometimes it was a snide remark about evangelical Christians. Or maybe he would speak in some kind of "televangelist voice" or complain that preachers were just out for money. Even though Jimmy was strong in his faith, this was a little bit much. It seemed like his teacher delighted in agitating the Christians in his classes. What was his problem anyway?

As soon as class started, Mr. Jurzack said that he had a great question he wanted to begin the class with. He stood in front of Jimmy's desk and said, "You Christians believe that your God can do anything, right?" With apprehension, Jimmy said, "Yes." Mr. Jurzack was ready to pounce, "So then, if God can do anything, can he make a rock so big that he can't lift it?" The teacher smiled with smug satisfaction as some of Jimmy's classmates snickered. Jimmy felt trapped.

———

Anyone who has ever been in Jimmy's place can relate. There is often

A Journey Through The Gospels

some intellectual smart aleck who thinks it's his job to make believers look foolish. The Sadducees thought they would do that to Jesus. But Jesus is not Jimmy. Jesus always had an answer. He showed their question about the seven wives to be foolish, but he also showed them something more.

The problem of the Sadducees was that they didn't understand the kingdom of Heaven, or the power of God. Jesus told these intellectual wise guys they didn't understand the nature of God. *But regarding the fact that the dead rise again, have you not read in the book of Moses, in the passage about the burning bush, how God spoke to him, saying, 'I am the God of Abraham, and the God of Isaac, and the God of Jacob?' He is not the God of the dead, but of the living; you are greatly mistaken"* (Mark 12:26-27).

God is not a God of the dead, nor is He dead. God is a living God who gives life in every situation. What is the need you have today? Don't let the mistaken ideas of the world trap you in misguided thinking. The Living God will bring life to you!

Let's Pray:
*God you are alive! Thank you for working to bring
new life to me. Help me to see you working
in every situation. You are good!
In Jesus' name, Amen!*

(By the way, the answer to Mr. Jurzack's question is: No, God cannot make a rock so big that He cannot lift it. You and I can discuss why that is the correct answer by dropping me a line at thollis@ctvn.org. I'd love to hear from you.)

100 Days With Jesus

Day 51
Mark 13 — ARE WE IN THE END TIMES?

> *"Tell us, when will these things be, and what will be the sign when all these things are going to be fulfilled?"* - Mark 13:4

I grew up in the 1970's. It was a great era. It was a time of bell bottoms, classic rock, and long hair. Spiritually, it was a time of "Jesus People," charismatics, and gospel tracts. In the 70's I began to follow Christ closely, got baptized in water and with the Holy Spirit. I found my calling, and met my wife. Great decade.

Another thing the 70's was famous for was the End Times. There were sermons, movies, TV shows, tracts, and a multitude of books about the End Times. One of my favorite ministries at that time was called *Last Days Ministries* (still in operation today). There were even songs about the end times.

We all believed that the Rapture could happen any day. We would all rise in the sky in the "twinkling of an eye." But it didn't happen in the 70's or the 80's. I began to get disenchanted with the whole idea that the End Times were imminent. I decided to just concentrate on loving Jesus and preaching the gospel, and let the Lord worry about the End Times. I didn't buy any more End Times

A Journey Through The Gospels

books (especially *88 Reasons Why Jesus Will Return In 1988*). It's worked out well for me.

However…

It began to dawn on me that Jesus told us to be aware of the signs of the times. "*What I say to you I say to all, 'Be on the alert!'*" (Mark 13:37). Whole chapters of the gospels are devoted to the End Times, including this one. If Jesus is concerned about the End Times, then I suppose I need to be, also. I won't be making any predictions on the date of the Rapture (Hmmm… *21 Reasons Why Jesus Will Return In 2021* has a nice ring to it), but I will keep my eyes open.

Let's Pray:
Dear Lord, keep me aware of the signs of the times.
Let me preach the gospel at all times.
Let me dwell close to your heart always.
In your name I pray, Amen!

100 Days With Jesus

Day 52
Mark 14   ## THE PHARISEE

> *Some began to spit at Him, and to blindfold Him, and to beat Him with their fists, and to say to Him, "Prophesy!" And the officers received Him with slaps in the face.* - Mark 14:65

The Pharisee felt anger seething through his bones! Who was this man to claim that He was the son of God? From his seat in the back he ran forward with all his might. He felt the oppression of the Romans and the hope of the true messiah who would deliver them. This ragged prophet was no messiah. How dare He! He was false! He needed to be stopped and His misguided followers rounded up. We have to stamp this out! We have to worship the true God, not this man! He swung his fist in fury and connected to the face of Jesus.

Jesus saw the man running toward Him. They had never spoken, but He remembered seeing him on the street. With the eyes of God, Jesus saw the Pharisee's rage, misguided though it was. He looked deeper into the dark heart of this man. He saw hate, hypocrisy and error. Looking deeper still, Jesus saw the pain, the sin, the separation from the Father. He saw the enemy using every wound to fuel the man's rage and confuse his picture of God. Jesus saw the twisted soul and broken spirit that had erected a barrier between himself and God's love. As the Pharisee's punch landed, Jesus felt forgiveness well up in His heart.

A Journey Through The Gospels

We know from the scriptures that Jesus came to seek and to save that which was lost. Yet we forget He came for all, for all have sinned. We see someone we love who needs Jesus, and we know that Jesus desires to save them. But we struggle to feel God's love for the criminal, the bold sinner, the blasphemer, and the self-righteous. But God loves the whole world. There is no place God's love doesn't reach. There is no heart so dark God doesn't desire to rescue it.

How little we really understand the love of God! It is so much deeper and fuller of grace than human love could ever be. The Pharisee in our story above doesn't deserve Jesus' love or forgiveness, and yet forgiveness is there. If we could see the love of God, we would look upon the most beautiful object we had ever beheld. And we need that love.

This brings me to an interesting question: Who is the unnamed Pharisee in the story? It's simple really, if we think about it. Who has sinned? Who has rebelled against God? Who has rejected the Savior many times?

The Pharisee is me.

Let's Pray:
God, thank you for your love and mercy. Thank you that while I was away from God you still loved me. While I was an enemy of God you still died for me. Thank you for rescuing me from my sin and myself! In Jesus' name, Amen!

100 Days With Jesus

Day 53
Mark 15 **WAITING FOR THE KINGDOM**

Joseph of Arimathea came, a prominent member of the Council, who himself was waiting for the kingdom of God; and he gathered up courage and went in before Pilate, and asked for the body of Jesus. - Mark 15:43

*J*oseph sighed deeply. "I thought He might be the one," he said to himself as he considered the events of the day. Jesus' message had captured his heart. Jesus' miracles had been a sign to Joseph that Jesus was more than a prophet. "His message of love was radical! Too radical for the Sanhedrin." Joseph was ashamed of the Jewish leaders and their treatment of Jesus. He lamented how easily they rejected His message. Joseph had not been sure about Jesus at first, but the more he listened to Him the more he discerned the heart of God. And now? Now, He was dead. Joseph was a leader, too. He would at least treat Jesus with dignity in His death. He was in Pilate's antechamber presently. "We will lay Jesus in my family's tomb. Perhaps in His death His message will spread." A servant called for Joseph. He took a deep breath and entered in.

Our verse today says Joseph of Arimathea was a man who was "waiting for the kingdom of God." He was a rich man, a man of power and prestige, who surely thought that the kingdom would

A Journey Through The Gospels

come that way. He must have been firmly convinced that the Messiah would have glory greater than Solomon and have an army greater than all of the Roman legions. He likely fell in with other members of the council at first, rejecting Jesus as anything more than a desert teacher. I mean, Jesus was from Galilee! How could the Messiah come from that backwater? But Joseph was wiser than his brethren on the Council. As he observed Jesus, he became a follower. Perhaps the kingdom would come through this One.

We struggle to see God's kingdom, at times. We expect that God's plan will come in a nice package, just like we ordered it. But it doesn't come that way. It comes God's way. Jesus came into Jerusalem riding on a donkey, not in a chariot. The Pharisees missed the kingdom when He was standing right there. Joseph saw the true kingdom. Jesus has more glory than Solomon and more power than Rome, but only those with spiritual eyes will see it.

Has God's kingdom come upon you today? Ask Him. In ways small and large, quiet and loud, God will show you His love, His plan, and His purposes. Let him open your eyes today.

Let's Pray:
Father, there are times when I am blind to your kingdom.
Help me to see things today with the eyes of God!
In Jesus' name, Amen!

100 Days With Jesus

Day 54
Mark 16

A ROLLING STONE

They were saying to one another, "Who will roll away the stone for us from the entrance of the tomb?" Looking up, they saw that the stone had been rolled away, although it was extremely large. - Mark 16:3-4

The women coming to Jesus' tomb on Sunday morning did indeed have a problem, a LARGE problem. They knew there was a honking-big rock in the way of what they had come to do. Jesus had been buried in a tomb that long before had been cut directly out of the bedrock. A large round stone had been fashioned by stone masons to cover the doorway. It weighed several tons. A channel had been dug at the base of the doorway that continued up a small rise to the stone's resting spot. The stone was placed here waiting for its one-time use. After the body was placed in the tomb, the stone would be pushed down this short channel 'til it came to rest with a deep thud at the bottom, right in front of the door. The body would be sealed inside forever.

Mary Magdalene and the other Mary had good reason to be concerned. They needed to finish anointing Jesus' body for burial. They had cried about his death. They had despaired for the life of their Rabboni. They wanted to do what they thought they should do. They prepared the spices and oil and started on their short journey to the garden tomb. Then they remembered the stone.

A Journey Through The Gospels

Do you feel like there is an enormous roadblock in the way of fulfilling all God has for you? Do you feel like it will never move? These women were about to find out that all their concerns were unnecessary. When they got there, not only was the stone rolled away, but Jesus was alive! God's power could solve a little problem that seemed big, the Stone. Much more importantly, God can make that problem insignificant because of a greater deed, the Resurrection!

Don't let a stone stand in your way today. Like Mary and Mary, continue down the path to which God has directed you. These women continued to the garden even though they didn't know what they would do when they got there. They were faithful to their purpose and God showed them a higher purpose.

Let's Pray:
Jesus, help me to see past the problem
and see the Resurrected Christ.
Nothing can stand in my way as I follow you!
In your name, Amen!

100 Days With Jesus

Day 55
Luke 1

GENERATIONAL BLESSING

And His mercy is upon generation after generation toward those who fear Him. - Luke 1:50

Grandpa Amu worked diligently with the hands of a skilled craftsman. He was not a woodworker by trade, but his long experience in doing whatever was needed to be done served him well. He only had a few tools, but he worked them in every way possible. His hammer, chisel, saw and axe made cuts, small and big. Always, the cuts were precise, right where they needed to be.

Amu was building a bridge to cross the small stream on his family's property. Such a small flow of water, but a big problem to get over. Amu was helped by his son, and he wanted this bridge to last for him and his family. Each piece locked into the next one. Things fit so well that no nails were even used! Finally, the bridge was done. Grandpa Amu walked across it with his little grandson. In time, his grandson would build the next bridge.

Mary speaks in our scripture today and says that God's mercy will follow our descendants after us. What is this mercy? God's mercy is best defined as his lovingkindness. This is the quality of God which causes Him to feel for us in our difficulties, most importantly

A Journey Through The Gospels

in our sin. In fact, in Hebrews 4:15 it says, *For we do not have a high priest who cannot sympathize with our weaknesses.* The Lord feels for us with compassion for our situation. In Hosea he says, *My heart is turned over within Me, all My compassions are kindled* (Hosea 11:8b).

This compassion does more than cause God to feel sorry for us. God acts on our behalf. He moves in ways we need, at the moment we need it. We truly serve a great God! The greatest thing we can hand down to our sons and daughters is a relationship with God.

In our story, Grandpa Amu was thinking of future generations while he built his bridge. It is a joy to hand down a solid foundation physically and spiritually, to our descendants. As our scripture says, when we walk in the fear of the Lord, we ensure a spiritual footing for our family. Fear of the Lord really means "reverence." And we can walk in that reverence beginning today.

Let's Pray:
Lord, I haven't always walked close to you.
I haven't always had the proper reverence
for you in life and in front of my family.
Thank you, Lord, that today is a new day!
Help me begin to follow close to you.
In Jesus' name, Amen!

PS: Grandpa Amu really did build a bridge. You can watch it on YouTube.

100 Days With Jesus

Day 56
Luke 2 TREASURE OF THE HEART
___

And He said to them, "Why is it that you were looking for Me? Did you not know that I had to be in My Father's house?" - Luke 2:49

Mary ran frantically through the streets. Where could He be? She retraced the family's steps from a few days before. She asked friends if they had seen Him. She asked street vendors. No one had seen Jesus. She stopped to catch her breath for a moment and looking up, she saw Joseph coming to get her. "I found Him," he said, "He's all right." Mary's fear drained from her chest; she relaxed and silently thanked God. With a new calmness she asked, "Where is He, Joseph?" "He's in the temple, and you won't believe what's going on. Let me show you."

Mary had heard the word of the Lord from the angel Gabriel. Joseph had been told by God in a dream. The shepherds told them what the angels had said. Simeon and Anna had prophesied over Him in the temple. There was even a special star in the sky! Jesus was to be a great and special person. His name meant "God with us." He would save them from their sins. And yet they still didn't know who He really was.

To be fair to them, I'm sure they did not fully understand that Jesus was God in the flesh. How could they? Jesus Himself was growing

A Journey Through The Gospels

in the understanding of His mission. It says so in Luke 2:52: *And Jesus kept increasing in wisdom and stature, and in favor with God and men.* Jesus was fully God from the moment He was conceived, but He still had to grow in that knowledge as He grew as a man.

Have you ever received a word from God? Maybe a scripture, a teaching, or a prophecy that was directly for you. Perhaps you heard the still small voice of the Holy Spirit speak to you about something you would do or be. Let me say that these are precious words. They are worth more than gold. If you get light from the Holy Spirit, cherish and guard it.

Is that cherished word yet to be fulfilled? Are you confused or unsure of what the word even means? Don't give up. Mary and Joseph felt the same way about Jesus. But Mary did something else. She *"treasured all these things in her heart"* (Luke 2:51b). We need to do the same. Don't forget the word; God is going to bring it to pass.

Let's Pray:
*God, thank you that I get to have this
wonderful relationship with you!
Continue to lead me down life's path.
Thank you for the promises you have given to me.
I will trust in you. In Jesus' name, Amen!*

100 Days With Jesus

Day 57
Luke 3

WHEAT AND CHAFF

"His winnowing fork is in His hand to thoroughly clear His threshing floor, and to gather the wheat into His barn; but He will burn up the chaff with unquenchable fire." - Luke 3:17

Let's say Queen Elizabeth is coming over to your house for dinner. What would you do? You would clean every corner of your living room, trim the shrubs outside, and throw away the expired food in your refrigerator. You would buy a new set of clothes to wear and make sure everyone looked their best. You would want to make a good impression. Well, someone far greater than the queen was coming to Israel, and John the Baptist wants the people to get ready, spiritually ready.

Israel was a nation of farmers, and throughout its entire history, farm analogies are used to describe spiritual things. John uses one here. In those days, farmers would lay the harvested grain on the ground and beat it. This broke up the heads of grain so that the chaff (inedible part) could be separated. Doesn't sound like much fun for the grain, does it? But there was one more step: the farmer would use a pitchfork to throw the grain into air, and the wind would carry all the chaff away. Only the good and pure grain would be left.

John tells them that the Coming One will baptize them with the

A Journey Through The Gospels

Holy Spirit and fire. This was going to be a grand entrance by the Messiah. He was not coming to be on the sidelines. He was going to take over, and He was looking for those with prepared hearts. The Messiah was going to "winnow the chaff" out of the hearts of His followers. John's sermon is one of repentance, which means to "turn around" and head in another direction, away from sin and toward God. John is using this platform to speak of the coming Messiah. He wants everyone to be ready for His arrival.

We are the grain in this story, and we will have this winnowing process in our own lives. First, all false believers will be separated out. Then the true believers will have the "chaff" of their hearts winnowed. Perhaps you feel the Holy Spirit doing that to you already. Jesus wants to be first in your life. He wants the spiritual chaff out. Then the fire will come!

Let's pray:
*Lord, help me to set aside anything that
gets in the way of my devotion to you.
Fill me with your fire! In your name, Amen!*

100 Days With Jesus

Day 58
Luke 4 ## AN OPPORTUNE TIME

Jesus, full of the Holy Spirit, returned from the Jordan and was led around by the Spirit in the wilderness for forty days, being tempted by the devil. And He ate nothing during those days, and when they had ended, He became hungry. - Luke 4:1-2

*H*ave you ever spent days or even weeks fasting and had a great spiritual breakthrough? Nah…me neither. Don't get me wrong, I'm glad for everyone who has been blessed by a fast. It just doesn't seem to work that well for me. I'm sure the problem is in the mirror.

Anyhoo...

Jesus does a fast right before He starts His ministry. Forty days without food! But look at that first phrase in our scripture, "*Jesus, full of the Holy Spirit.*" It wasn't abstaining from food or even the mortification of His flesh that was the key. It was the fullness of the Holy Spirit empowering Him. Jesus was going to need that power. The devil was on the prowl. You may think that the devil was no match for Jesus, and you would be right. But remember, Jesus was a human man in a weakened physical state.

The devil tempts Him with three things: Doubt about who He was: "*If you are the Son of God.*" Power: "*Worship me and I'll give you the world.*" Foolishly Testing God: "*Throw yourself down.*" Jesus is ready with strong scriptural rebukes for the devil, and the devil departs. However, there is an ominous warning in Luke 4:13,

A Journey Through The Gospels

When the devil had finished every temptation, he left Him until an opportune time (emphasis mine). Sometimes the devil sees our level of commitment to stand against him, and he departs. We may be riding high on a spiritual plane, and victories are coming easily. Everything is going great, and the devil sees he can't get at us.

However, we don't always stay so spiritually sharp. A few weeks or months later, you walk out your front door, and the devil's leaning against the lamp post in your front yard. "Remember me?" he says. And the attacks begin. Will you be ready? Will you have victory?

Yes, you will. Jesus overcame the temptations in the wilderness leaving an example for your victory. He is completely committed to your success in this never-ending battle.

Hang on to the Solid Rock of Jesus Christ today. Don't let the world wear you down. Don't let down your spiritual guard. Chase that lamppost guy out of your front yard when you see him!

Let's Pray:
Father, I'm feeling great right now.
The victories are coming and my spirit is strong.
Keep me close to you and full of the Holy Spirit.
Alert me to any sneak attacks from the enemy!
In Jesus' name, Amen!

100 Days With Jesus

Day 59
Luke 5

MORE THAN HE BARGAINED FOR

Seeing their faith, He said, "Friend, your sins are forgiven you."
- Luke 5:20

The young man looked at Jesus with eyes full of expectation. He had heard of the great miracles that this prophet from Galilee had done. He needed a miracle, too. Lame since birth, he had no prospects. No way to earn a living, no way to provide for a family. No woman to call his wife. He seemed to be headed for a life as a beggar.

What was worse was the scorn some people heaped upon him and his family. They said it was God's punishment. They said there must be sin in the parents' lives. Why else would God bring such judgment? People who smiled to his face talked about him behind his back. These whispers brought a cutting pain to the young man's soul.

Praise God for his friends. They were a good bunch. They were fun and they made him feel like one of the guys. Just yesterday he heard Jesus was in town. He said, "It would be great to see Him." His friends seized on that and told the paralytic that they would take him to see Jesus. The rest of the story is told in the Gospel of Luke: Four friends climb on the roof; They tear up the shingles and lower their friend by ropes, right next to Jesus.

A Journey Through The Gospels

Jesus looks at the man, then looks up at his friends and then, with a smile in His eyes, back at the man. The man gets the best gift from Jesus that any person could ever get, *"Friend, your sins are forgiven you."* The man, still paralyzed, felt a rush of cleansing over his soul. He felt like a new man in his old body. He didn't really hear the discussion that was taking place just then. He had peace and joy. It was okay if he didn't get healed; he was healed on the inside.

Wait... Jesus was saying something else to him.

What's that? Rise and walk?! His body felt electrified! It was like a dream. What's that? Rise and go home? Take my stretcher? The man jumped up! He looked at Jesus! He praised God! He went leaping and shouting with his friends all the way home! He was no longer an outcast, and he was no longer a sinner. The man had wanted a healing, but he got more than he bargained for: he got a new life!

The Bible says that Jesus does all things well. He will do that for you today, and do more than you ever imagined. Whatever you need, trust Him today.

Let's Pray:
Father, I ask in Jesus' name that you restore me.
Do the deep work in me, Lord. Do your complete work.
Praise your holy name! Amen!

100 Days With Jesus

Day 60
Luke 6 ROCK OR SAND?

Everyone who comes to Me and hears My words and acts on them, I will show you whom he is like: he is like a man building a house, who dug deep and laid a foundation on the rock; and when a flood occurred, the torrent burst against that house and could not shake it, because it had been well built. - Luke 6:47-48

My daughter Ashley is in the resort industry. Her work lands her in some of the most beautiful and fun places in the world. For a time, she had a job at Kiawah Island resort in Charleston, South Carolina. It has a stunning hotel called "The Sanctuary." We stayed there for a few nights, which we would not normally have been able to afford. Ashley's discount got us there on the cheap. Way to go, Ashley!

The hotel sits right on the beach, and we spent a good bit of time there. We rode our bikes up and down the length of it. There were gorgeous beachfront homes all along the way, more like "beachfront mansions," really. There had been a very bad storm just several months before we arrived. We noticed something. Every property had a ramp and walkway to the beach. These were made out of deck wood, and there was a consistent theme: nearly every one of them had been destroyed by the bad weather.

Interestingly, none of the homes had been badly damaged. Why was that? It was because they had been built with solid foundations.

A Journey Through The Gospels

The storm, as bad as it was, had not affected them too much. Maybe a few shingles here or there; but otherwise, they stood strong. However, the ramps had been built on the sand. They were torn up easily.

Jesus uses a similar illustration in our scripture today. Building on the rock means acting on the word of Jesus. If we do this, we will have a foundation of double-thick concrete set on the bedrock of life. We will have everything we need to make it through life's roughest weather. However, if we hear Jesus' words and don't act on them, it will be like living on the beach in a tent during a monsoon!

Have you built that strong foundation? It begins by knowing God's word, but it doesn't stop there. As you grow in your knowledge of God, He will move you into effective places for Him. Be sure to hear and act! God will give you the open door and the strength to walk through it.

Let's Pray:
*Lord Jesus, you have faithfully delivered
your word to me. I know you will give me the will
and the way to act upon it. Keep my vision
clear as I follow after you.
In your name, Amen!*

100 Days With Jesus

Day 61
Luke 7

SHE LOVED MUCH

And there was a woman in the city who was a sinner; and when she learned that He was reclining at the table in the Pharisee's house, she brought an alabaster vial of perfume. - Luke 7:37

The woman snuck up along with some guests entering the house. She would never be invited to such a grand home. "Well, not officially," she sadly mused. There was no humor in that comment. Her conscience troubled her deeply as she thought of all the men she had led astray. They had led her astray too, of course. Both parties were guilty, she knew, but there was no time for that now. She was too attracted to this prophet from Galilee. She knew men, and she knew that He was more than a man. She wanted to come and honor Him, but what could she do?

She got the only expensive thing that she owned. She carried it into the house, having already dealt with grief over how she had acquired it. Her sins were coming strong upon her mind now. She was close to the holiest man that she had ever known. Jesus seemed to radiate purity. She was anything but pure. It was impossible for her to stand in His presence. The weight of her sins forced her to the ground.

She crawled over to where Jesus was sitting and cracked open the vial of perfume. A beautiful fragrance filled the air, but something

A Journey Through The Gospels

stronger was there, too. There was a presence of God in the room. She poured the costly liquid on the Savior's feet, and then the flood gates opened. Tears flowed like streams from her eyes onto his feet. She began to wipe them off with her hair. Jesus didn't stop her.

Suddenly she felt light, like the weight of a thousand bricks had been taken off her shoulders. She looked up into Jesus' eyes. Holiness flowed out of them to her, but also something else: Love. She had not experienced love since she was a child. She knew she didn't deserve it, but Jesus showed her that she did.

Now she became aware of her surroundings. The guests were watching it all. She hoped the homeowner wouldn't throw her out. Jesus was speaking to him. She barely heard what He said, but she did hear these words: *Her sins, which are many, have been forgiven, for she loved much* (Luke 7:47). A thrill of joy went through her whole body. She was accepted! She was forgiven! She had not even dared to hope for so much. She sat up. Jesus motioned for her to sit with His disciples, and He began to teach.

Let's Pray:
Jesus, let me honor you the way this woman did.
Let me realize that those who are forgiven much,
love much. Thank you for your forgiveness!

100 Days With Jesus

Day 62
Luke 8   *WHO TOUCHED ME?*

> *And a woman who had a hemorrhage for twelve years, and could not be healed by anyone, came up behind Him and touched the fringe of His cloak, and immediately her hemorrhage stopped. And Jesus said, "Who is the one who touched Me?"* - Luke 8:43-45a

The Apostle Paul in the Book of Acts says of the Athenians, "*I perceive that you are a religious people.*" The same could be said of America and its great religious heritage. A study in 2012 found that there were 384,000 congregations in the United States! What an incredible number! It would seem that the need for evangelism is nearly over. Everyone is saved already, right?

No, not really. Not even close. A large number of churches, while not a bad thing, is not an indication of widespread salvation. Some people go to church out of habit, some out of duty. Some churches are nearly empty. Something more is needed. What could that be?

We have an indication in our scriptural passage today. In Luke 8, Jesus had just returned from a mission trip to the other side of the Sea of Galilee. The multitudes were waiting for Him as He returned. Crowds pressed in upon Him. People were jostling Him from all sides. His disciples almost had to be bodyguards to keep the people off Him. But suddenly someone "touched" Jesus.

A Journey Through The Gospels

Jesus recognized immediately that divine power had gone out from Him. It was a woman who needed a healing. She had reached a place where no one else had. Others had come to see the show. Perhaps they were honestly seeking truth, but they hadn't reached it yet. She had. Jesus stopped and spoke to her. She got her healing and a lot more. She had an encounter with the Savior.

Jesus is never looking for ritual worship. He is never looking for mere tradition or observance. He is passionate about an encounter with you. Think about that for a moment: we all know that we need a relationship with Jesus, but Jesus wants a relationship with us! It's not recorded in the Bible, but I know that the woman who touched Jesus was never the same.

Today is a beginning. Reach out to Jesus with all your strength. Don't let distractions get in the way. Don't let past disappointments define your life. Jesus is looking for those who will touch the hem of His garment.

Let's Pray:
Jesus, I need you today! Let me touch you.
Give me faith and tenacity.
Help me to get past the distractions.
In your name, Amen!

100 Days With Jesus

Day 63
Luke 9

UNASHAMED

For whoever is ashamed of Me and My words, the Son of Man will be ashamed of him when He comes in His glory, and the glory of the Father and of the holy angels. - Luke 9:26

Joe's heart skipped a beat as the man approached him. What did Joe think he was doing out here on a street corner passing out gospel tracts, anyway? He wasn't Billy Graham. He was shy by nature. His first inclination was to crawl into a manhole and pull the lid over top of himself. But Jesus had told His disciples to preach the gospel, so here he was. "Lord," Joe thought, "You called the wrong man! I'm no evangelist!"

The oncoming man was mere steps away now. Joe swallowed hard and handed him a tract. The man grumbled something and went on his way. "God bless you," Joe said outwardly, but inside he moaned. "Ugh! This isn't working very well, Lord!" He longed for the outreach to be over.

Just then the presence of the Lord surrounded Joe. He felt the Holy Spirit say, "Faithful man. You bless Me when you share My love! Be at peace." Joe was overwhelmed, and he felt his heart change. He was still shy, but he would gladly share the love of God with anyone who passed by.

A young lady came up to Joe. He smiled, gave her a tract and invited

A Journey Through The Gospels

her to church. Her face was loaded with care. Joe asked her if he could pray for her. She said yes, and the Spirit descended. After a powerful prayer, she looked at Joe through her tears and said, "What time does your church start, again?" Joe smiled, and the peace of God overcame him.

There are times I have struggled with the words of Jesus in today's verse. Like Joe, I'm shy by nature. It always troubled me that Jesus seemed to be saying that to truly be His disciple I had to be bold and outgoing. But that is not what Jesus was saying.

Paul said in Romans *"For I am not ashamed of the gospel, for it is the power of God unto salvation."* We should never be ashamed of God's Word and His salvation message. This doesn't mean that we are all cut out to be street evangelists. We can reach people with the gospel in many ways: acts of love, notes of truth; give a hug, bake a cake, invite them to your house for a Bible study. All of these can lead to an understanding of, and opening for, the gospel.

So, to apply our verse for today: Don't be ashamed of Christ's words, and find a way to share them with others. You've got this!

Let's Pray:
Jesus, you have the words of life.
Let me never be ashamed of them. Give me the
boldness and creativity I need to share your love
with someone today! In your name, Amen!

100 Days With Jesus

Day 64
Luke 10 — **THE THREE**

At that very time, He rejoiced greatly in the Holy Spirit and said, "I praise Thee, O Father, Lord of heaven and earth." - Luke 10:21a (NAS)

What a tremendous relationship the Trinity has! Think of the best relationship you have ever had. Maybe it was your spouse, or a best friend, or a sibling or cousin that you just couldn't wait to spend time with. You were so close to them that they seemed to know what was in your heart before you said it. They could make you laugh, cry and rejoice. They put their arm around you and let you lean on them whenever life was tough. They were the perfect friend. At least, it seemed that way.

Maybe things didn't work out with that one. Relationships can become cold. They can get tangled with emotions and disappointments. Maybe that one moved away, or you graduated from school and they weren't there anymore. Perhaps there was a misunderstanding, or maybe they really hurt you. Maybe you hurt them. Sin brings devastation to our most cherished relationships.

That has never happened to the Trinity. In our verse today, in the space of fourteen words, the perfect relationship of the three members of this communion is expressed. *"He (Jesus) rejoiced greatly in the Holy Spirit and said, 'I praise Thee, O Father.'"*

A Journey Through The Gospels

Notice how all three are present at the culmination of this time of ministry. The Three are like that. They like to show up for things! They were there at Jesus' baptism. Remember, the Spirit descended and the Father spoke. They were present at the crowning creation of God. *"Let Us make man in Our image,"* they said. The Three who are One was there to greet Adam.

They are there for you today, too. They were there when you were born. They rejoiced greater than any earthly parent to see you grow. They were there at your happiest times, and they ached for you at your lowest valleys. They, the Three who are One, rejoiced at your salvation. They couldn't wait to usher you into their relationship. They knew that you would now understand the joy they had in knowing you.

C.S. Lewis said that "Joy is the serious business of Heaven." Joy is the outcome of a relationship with God the Father, God the Son, and God the Holy Spirit. Do you have that joy? The Three want to give it to you today.

Let's Pray:
Father, Son, and Holy Spirit open the windows of
heaven and pour on me your joy today.
Thank you for bringing me into the center of your heart.
In your presence is fullness of joy!
In Jesus' name, Amen!

100 Days With Jesus

Day 65
Luke 11   *Herb Garden in a Cemetery*

But woe to you Pharisees! For you pay tithe of mint and rue and every kind of garden herb, and yet disregard justice and the love of God; but these are the things you should have done without neglecting the others. - Luke 11:42

One of the great doctrines of the Christian faith is that Jesus is fully God. He was divine, one with God the Father, and part of the Holy Trinity. However, it is also a great truth and a foundation of Christianity that Jesus was fully man. He came as God clothed in flesh. The term we use to describe this quality of Jesus is He is "God Incarnate."

Since He was God, he had miraculous power and wisdom. Since He was man, He had needs. He got tired, and He had to eat. He was also very emotional at times. He even seemed to get discouraged or at least exasperated. But it was not all gloomy. A prophecy about Him in Psalms 45 says that He would be anointed *"with the oil of gladness above thy fellows."* Jesus was a happy, joy-filled person!

But boy, could Jesus get angry when He had to. Just ask the money changers in the temple. Of course, His greatest ire was directed at the religious leaders of the day.

Jesus didn't spare any words when He spoke to the Pharisees. In Luke 11, Jesus really puts the wood to them. He says that they are

A Journey Through The Gospels

clean cups on the outside, but full of robbery and wickedness inside. In other places in scripture, Jesus calls them whitewashed tombs! Perhaps His most stinging rebuke is in our passage today. The Pharisees sure did pay their tithes, didn't they? Every single bit of income was calculated and tithed upon, even herbs. They did this outward goodness, while harboring evil intentions and thoughts in their heart.

God told the prophet Samuel that man looks on the outside but He looks at the heart. He is not interested in accepting our sacrifices, our fasting, our offerings, or our tithes when our hearts are far from Him.

Our challenge today is to draw close to God. The Pharisees had an herb garden, but it was with them in the cemetery. Tithing on it did no good. Much better to have a pure heart and a growing relationship with God.

Let's Pray:
God, let my sacrifices never hide an evil heart.
Help me to clean the inside of the cup,
so that I can serve you from a pure heart.
Always. In Jesus' name, Amen!

100 Days With Jesus

Day 66
Luke 12   *It Will Be Given You*

> *When they bring you before the synagogues and the rulers and the authorities, do not worry about how or what you are to speak in your defense, or what you are to say; for the Holy Spirit will teach you in that very hour what you ought to say.* - Luke 12:11-12

*D*iotrephes sat up and stretched. Sleeping on the floor of a cold cell didn't do much for his joints. This was his third night since being arrested for preaching the gospel in the town square. "How strange," he thought, "all I want to do is share with them the incredible peace I've found in Jesus. It's good news! But for the joy of this good news, I'm being persecuted." He scratched his head in amazement at the hardness of men's hearts.

Diotrephes began to pray. His mind was drawn to the teaching of the elders that he had learned in the early days. Most of the elders were gone now, four decades since the resurrection of the Lord. They said that John the Beloved Apostle was still alive, but it had been thirty years since Diotrephes had heard him teach. He remembered something the apostle told him that Jesus had said.

Jesus promised that we would be persecuted. He also said that the Holy Spirit would teach them what to say when they were called before the authorities. "Well, that's about to happen, so I'll trust in you, Lord Jesus."

The jailer called out to him, "Get up, atheist!" Diotrephes thought

A Journey Through The Gospels

it funny that they called him an "atheist." It was because he taught that the Roman gods didn't exist. How much he wanted them to know the true and living God! The jailer bound his hands and rudely brought him before the magistrate.

The magistrate was an overly self-important local official, placed by the Romans to judge small cases. He stared down at the dirty man before him. Diotrephes was called forward and charged with being an atheist. "What do you have to say for yourself, atheist?"

Diotrephes felt a surge of power through his body. He was closer to the Holy Spirit than ever before. There was a lightness in his chest that he couldn't explain. He felt the Spirit of God giving him words of life. Suddenly, he opened his mouth and began to speak.

As followers of Christ, we can always be sure of having every word we need, everything we need, when we need it. It won't come a moment sooner.

Let's Pray:
Lord Jesus, at times I've doubted that you
would be there for me. Help me to remember your
promise to be with me always,
even until the end of the world.
Thank you, Lord! Amen!

100 Days With Jesus

Day 67
Luke 13   THE NARROW WAY

> *Strive to enter through the narrow door; for many, I tell you, will seek to enter and will not be able.* - Luke 13:24

Cyrus seemed to be walking in a fog. He stumbled a bit and skinned a knee, but he kept on moving. He was alone, but he could hear voices a bit off in the distance, on the other side of the fog. The path climbed up a little, and Cyrus huffed and puffed his way up to a little clearing.

As he came out into the clearing, he saw an overlook behind a railing. The fog was gone now. He walked there and leaned over the railing to take in the scene.

Below him, not so very far away, was a broad, well-made highway. It was paved with beautiful slate-blue flagstones. There were polished granite curbs along the sides of the highway. In the center ran a grass median at least 40 feet wide, and every so often there was a glorious fountain bubbling with clear water that formed a stream in the middle of the median. The sun was high and shining.

But there was something more: PEOPLE! There were people everywhere! They were walking along the road in their finest clothes. Some were in silver carriages pulled by horses. Families were having picnics on the median. Others waded in the fountains.

A Journey Through The Gospels

As soon as they finished their picnic, they got back on the road and kept walking.

As Cyrus was taking in this scene, he noticed something else. Every so often a crude path branched off and met up with the path Cyrus was on. People seemed to stumble upon the path. Some left the path as soon as they found it. Others struggled mightily to find the narrow way. When they found it, they rejoiced. Their old friends from the highway called to them to come back. The friends gave up soon though and went back to the multitude. Some of the saddest people searched for the path, but could never seem to find it.

Cyrus looked up and saw the destination of the highway. Every walker was oblivious to the fact that in a few short yards the road fell into a fiery canyon. Over it was a name: "Destruction." Cyrus tried to yell and warn the walkers but they couldn't hear him.

Cyrus woke up.

He knelt by the bed and prayed. "Father, let me never take your salvation for granted. Thank you that I am on the narrow way, the way that leads to life. Walk with me, Lord Jesus, and help me to lead others to your path. In your name, Amen!"

May your prayer and mine be the same as Cyrus'!

100 Days With Jesus

Day 68
Luke 14 — ## HONOR — A CHRISTIAN STORY

> *For everyone who exalts himself will be humbled,*
> *and he who humbles himself will be exalted.* - Luke 14:11

Bud laid aside his mop and bucket one last time. He had been janitor at the First Baptist Church for the past 37 years, and today was his last day. He looked almost lovingly at his little supply closet, with the mops and brooms all neatly in a row and its slop sink in the corner. "Funny" he thought, "that someone could get attached to a closet." But he fought back a tear as he closed and locked the door.

He rushed home to change and pick up Emily. Today was a special dinner to honor Pastor Brookes' 25th anniversary at the church, and he didn't want to be late. He and Emily jumped in Bud's pickup truck and headed over to the town armory where the event was to be held. "The mayor is supposed to be here tonight," Emily said. "And they are even going to read a proclamation from the governor." *That's good,* Bud thought. Pastor Brookes was a faithful servant of God, and he was glad to see him honored.

Emily and Bud got there about five minutes before the start of the event. They chose some inconspicuous seats at the back. This was just right for Bud. The festivities had just started when Pastor Brookes got up and walked to the mic. He did the last thing that anyone expected. Motioning to the back of the hall, he said, "Bud and Emily Johnson, please come up here. You're in the wrong seats." With much prodding and handclapping from the audience, Bud sheepishly walked

A Journey Through The Gospels

up on the dais with Emily, where there were two seats next to the mayor. Before he could sit down, the pastor called Bud over. "Folks, I have known many faithful servants of God in my time, but one stands above all. Bud Johnson has devoted his life to the service of the kingdom of God. Without fanfare, without acclaim, Bud has cleaned, scrubbed, and polished every square inch of First Baptist Church. In 37 years, Bud has never sought recognition. In fact, he's avoided it as much as he could. But tonight, this night is for you, Bud!"

The place erupted into applause, and tears streamed down Emily's face. Bud sheepishly sat in the place of honor at the head table. He was in a bit of a daze. There was a great meal, but he had a hard time eating at first, but he began to settle in. After dessert, a dozen or more people got up and shared their stories of Bud's faithfulness. They spoke of his great work, but they said more than that. They talked of his joy and kind words, his smiles and firm handshakes. And all of them shared that his prayers got them through tough times. In short, they shared about a man who lived like Jesus. Pastor Brookes had the final word. His message was from the teaching of Christ, "The greatest among you shall be the servant of all."

Finally, the night was over. Bud shook his last handshake. He and Emily got in the truck and drove home. As they finished their prayers, Bud's head hit the pillow. "Thanks Lord; it's been a great run." Somewhere in the depths of his heart, Bud heard, "There is more to come, O faithful man." With that, Bud smiled and fell asleep thinking of the future.

> ***Let's Pray:*** Father, help me to never seek the limelight, but to always walk in Your light. Help me to be a faithful servant of God and others. In Jesus' name, Amen!

100 Days With Jesus

Day 69
Luke 15

SENSE AND SENSIBILITIES

"But when he came to his senses, he said, 'How many of my father's hired men have more than enough bread, but I am dying here with hunger!'"
- Luke 15:17

There is a famous quote that I really like. I feel it has the ring of truth to it. Here it is: *"There is nothing so uncommon as common sense."* This saying has a "home-spun" quality to it. That's what I like about it. It sounds like something your dad might have said to you, or that Harry Truman or Ronald Reagan might have said to the nation. It just feels right.

So just what is common sense? The dictionary defines common sense as "sound and prudent judgment based on a simple perception of the situation or facts." That seems like a good working definition for our topic today. Today we are speaking about the Prodigal Son.

The prodigal son had anything but common sense. He wanted his inheritance, and he wanted to party. He got his money and proceeded to lose his mind. But then, after all the money and friends and fun were gone, the Bible says, "he began to be in need." Do you know that need can be a necessary component of us coming to our senses, of restoring common sense to our thinking?

A Journey Through The Gospels

God, our loving Heavenly Father, will use need in our lives. He will let need speak to us. This means letting us experience hardship. No parent wants their child to experience difficulty and pain. But sometimes that is the only thing that gets our attention. The prodigal son's need became the cold slap in the face that brought him to the place God wanted him to be.

And what was the result? He came to his senses. He decided to return to his father, maybe he could be a servant, he thought. He was about to get more than he bargained for. You see, the son still didn't know his Father well enough. He didn't know that he would be completely forgiven and restored. Not only was he restored, he also got to know his father in a deeper way. His father was better than he knew.

How about us? Have we "gotten it" yet? Has a need driven you to seek God? I'm sure that each of us have experienced such a time in our lives. Thankfully we don't have to stay in that dark place.

Seek God with all your heart, and see how good He can be. God is a better Father than we know!

Let's Pray:
Father, my need has driven me to seek your face.
Help me, Lord. Provide what I need
and show me your goodness.
I love you, Lord!

100 Days With Jesus

Day 70
Luke 16

LITTLE AND BIG

He who is faithful in a very little thing is faithful also in much; and he who is unrighteous in a very little thing is unrighteous also in much. - Luke 16:10

Billy pushed the lawn mower one long last stretch of yard. He switched it off, and it sputtered a bit until it stopped. Man, it was hot out! Sweat poured off of Billy as he tugged the mower back over to Mrs. McHenry's garage to put it away. He was glad to be done.

Just then he noticed it! A piece of lawn in the side yard that he had missed. *Ugh, he didn't want to do any more!* That part of the yard was behind an apple tree, and Mrs. McHenry wouldn't even see it unless she went back there. He could just wait until next week. The grass wasn't even that long…

Suddenly the mower roared back to life. Billy pushed it behind the apple tree and finished the job, albeit a bit grumpily. Unknown to Billy, Mrs. McHenry was watching the entire time.

There are times in our life that we have been given a task we'd rather not do. We find it uncomfortable or hard. There can be a temptation to cut corners, to not finish the job correctly, or to not finish it at all. Sometimes we want to quit and do something else.

A Journey Through The Gospels

Thankfully for Mrs. McHenry's lawn, Billy overcame his desire to quit.

This can be especially difficult if we feel the job is below us or unimportant. We feel called to great things, important stuff, the up-front ministry. But God seems to be taking forever to get us there. "God, why did you call me here?" we might say. We didn't want to be a stagehand or mechanic or "Janitor for Jesus." But God really does know what He is doing. He is using the time and tasks that are in front of us to train us.

"Do not despise the day of small beginnings" it says in Zechariah 4. We should never look down on the place we find ourselves or the work that we are given to do. What we need to do is glorify God with the good work that we do. Every great person, every successful man or woman has started low and worked their way up. They did this by doing a good job on the work in front of them.

One more interesting point: Jesus spoke our verse today (Luke 16:10) in the middle of a teaching about the use of money. I find it fascinating that Jesus felt that money was a small thing. Real riches are something so much more!

Let's Pray:
God, thank you for the work I have been given to do.
Whether you move me on or
You have called me here for a long time,
let me always do a job that will glorify your name!
In Jesus' name I pray, Amen!

100 Days With Jesus

Day 71
Luke 17

A PUNCH IN THE FACE!

"And if he sins against you seven times a day, and returns to you seven times, saying, 'I repent,' forgive him." - Luke 17:4

Jesus was a really radical teacher. He was constantly saying things that blew away the Pharisees and challenged His followers. Whether it was "Love your enemies" or "The rocks will cry out" or "Eat my flesh," Jesus always left them amazed and sometimes bewildered. Some of His most challenging teachings are related to the area of forgiveness.

Jesus' entire ministry was one of forgiveness. Forgiveness was the reason He came and the reason He died. Before we get to today's verse, think of some of the other things Jesus said about forgiveness:
- "Forgive your brother 70 times 7."
- "If you won't forgive others, neither will you be forgiven."
- "Father, forgive them for they know not what they do."

These are all amazing statements from Jesus, and they are hard to live up to. But Jesus called those disciples, and modern-day disciples like you and me, to forgive. As hard as those teachings are, I think today's verse is the hardest to follow.

Let's play out this scenario. Your friend steals from you at 7:00 AM. He starts to feel bad about it, comes back at 7:30, and asks your forgiveness. You would be hurt that your friend would do such a thing, but being the good Christian that you are, you would forgive

A Journey Through The Gospels

him. Then at 8:00 he steals again, and at 8:30 asks your forgiveness again. In addition to locking your doors more securely, you are beginning to wonder about your friend, but you still forgive. Then at 9:00 he breaks a window to get in, since you locked your door, and steals again. He comes back at 9:30 and asks for forgiveness again. At this point you tell him, in King James English, all you really want to do is *"Punchest thee in thy face!"*

At least that's what I would tell him. Jesus tells the disciples to keep forgiving even to ridiculous extremes. Why? Because that is how God loves. God has forgiven us way more times than this, and when we forgive, we are most like Him.

The disciples' reaction was "Lord, increase our faith!" We need faith to do this. Jesus goes right into the "faith of a mustard seed" teaching. That kind of faith is small but powerful. It is all we need to see miracles. Miracles like forgiving our friend.

Let's Pray:
Heavenly Father, help me to be like you today.
Help me to forgive. I trust that you will give me
the grace and the faith to do it.
In Jesus' name, Amen!

PS: Let me be clear, under no circumstances should you allow yourself to be continually taken advantage of by another person. Even in our silly scenario above, forgiveness can be accompanied by proper boundaries. You are too important to Jesus to allow yourself to be abused.

100 Days With Jesus

Day 72
Luke 18 THE BOTHERER

There was a widow in that city, and she kept coming to him, saying, 'Give me legal protection from my opponent.' For a while he was unwilling; but afterward he said to himself, 'Even though I do not fear God nor respect man, yet because this widow bothers me, I will give her legal protection, otherwise by continually coming she will wear me out.' - Luke 18:3-5

We've all had that one person. They just couldn't let up. Maybe it was a child, a little person with an overactive mouth. "Are we there yet? Are we there yet?" Maybe it was someone you worked with or a neighbor. They were constantly asking you for something. Some people have a gift for tenacity in asking. Usually, we are not blessed by this "gift" of theirs. They can be a bother more than a blessing. (*Sorry if you are one. I still love you! Now, you may go.* ☺)

Jesus brings up this type of person in today's parable. Maybe we should take a moment to talk about parables. Parables resonate with us because we can relate to the people in them. As I said, we've all had the "botherer" in our lives, but we've also all had the unrighteous judge. There have been times that the red-tape and uncaring attitude of government officials is maddening.

All parables are memorable because of the unexpected turn they take. Jesus is using this one to illustrate prayer. As verse 1 of Luke 18 says, "*Now He was telling them a parable to show that at all*

A Journey Through The Gospels

times they ought to pray and not to lose heart." We are to learn a lesson here: keep praying! We are to be like the widow, going back again and again and again, asking the Lord for our answer. Maybe an old word would work here: beseech. We are to beseech the Lord, to ask him earnestly, fervently for what we need. We are the Botherer! At least, we should be.

Wait a minute! Does that make God the unrighteous judge? No, not exactly. Remember, this is a parable, not an allegory. Everything is not meant to match up perfectly like that. In fact, Jesus contrasts God and the unrighteous judge a couple of verses later: *"Now, will not God bring about justice for His elect who cry to Him day and night, and will He delay long over them? I tell you that He will bring about justice for them quickly"* (Luke 18:7-8a).

Yes, we need to pray consistently and fervently. But we also need to pray in faith and expectancy. If an unrighteous judge will be moved to action, how much sooner will Our Father be moved. God is better than we know!

Let's Pray:
God, I know you hear me when I pray.
Keep me close to you and consistent in prayer.
Keep me fervent as I wait to see you move.
In Jesus' name, Amen!

100 Days With Jesus

Day 73
Luke 19

GET TO THE YET

Go to the village ahead of you, and as you enter it, you will find a colt tied there, which no one has ever ridden. Untie it and bring it here. - Luke 19:30, (NIV)

Gerald the donkey was having a down day. He was just old enough to begin doing important work, but instead he was just standing around. All of his friends had started working, pulling hay wagons, taking the boss into town, even pulling the milk man's cart. Gerald wanted some real work to do, too!

Instead he was listless all day, penned up, waiting for who-knows-what. Didn't the boss see that he was almost full grown? Now he was tied up to this wretched post and he couldn't even walk around. "What a lousy day," he said to himself (as there were no other donkeys around to talk to).

Suddenly, two strange men approached and began to untie Gerald. The boss asked them what they were doing, and they just said a few words and the boss let him go! This was going to be an interesting day after all…

Sometimes, we can be exactly like Gerald the donkey. We know that we are created for something, but we can't quite figure out what that is. Or maybe you feel that you have a very good idea of your calling, but you just can't seem to get off the dime. And the wait is frustrating.

A Journey Through The Gospels

Let me encourage you. God does have a great plan for you! Remember this important scripture, "*For the vision is yet for the appointed time; It hastens toward the goal and it will not fail. Though it tarries, wait for it; for it will certainly come, it will not delay*" (Habakkuk 2:3).

There are some interesting action (or non-action) words here: *tarries* and *wait*. When we are moving toward a promise of God, these words will always be part of the process. There is another important word in this scripture: *yet*. The vision is *yet* for an appointed time. It's going to be a little while before we *get to the yet*.

Gerald finally got to the *yet*, but maybe it wasn't exactly what he thought. He had to go with strangers to a place he had never been. He had coats put on him on a hot day. And finally, he had a stranger sit on him. He had never had that happen before! He could have wanted to run away, but he stuck it out. He was getting to the *yet*, and it was coming soon.

Suddenly, people were everywhere, and they were shouting! This was finally what Gerald was created for. He never knew that he would be the one to usher the new King into Jerusalem.

It was worth the wait.

Let's Pray:
Father, don't let me run ahead of you or behind you.
Keep me always in the center of your will.
Help me to see the vision and wait for it.
In Jesus' name, Amen!

100 Days With Jesus

Day 74
Luke 20   NOW OR LATER
___

Everyone who falls on that stone will be broken to pieces; but on whomever it falls, it will scatter him like dust. - Luke 20:18

*T*here was a Fram oil filter commercial years ago that had the tagline, "You can pay me now, or you can pay me later." A mechanic was speaking to the viewer, lamenting how people didn't change their oil regularly. The results of not changing your oil regularly was your engine would break down and need to be rebuilt. Instead of a $20 oil change, you now had a $1,000 engine rebuild. The lesson we all needed to learn was *Pay me now, not later*.

In our chapter today, Jesus is speaking to some priests and scribes. The spiritual leaders of Israel were doing anything but leading the people spiritually. In fact, they were leading them astray. They were legalistic, proud, and uncaring, and yet this may not have been their most egregious fault. The worst thing about them was that they didn't recognize who Jesus was.

In the verse right before today's scripture, Jesus quotes an Old Testament prophecy about the Messiah: *But Jesus looked at them and said, "What then is this that is written: 'The stone which the builders rejected, this became the chief Cornerstone'* (Luke 20:17)? The Jews had been looking for the Messiah all of their lives, but when He was standing right in front of them, they rejected Him.

A Journey Through The Gospels

Then Jesus lowers the boom in verse 18. He was the Rock and everyone needs to fall on this rock and be broken. This applies to us. I've heard it said, sort of tongue-in-cheek, "Everyone is going to meet Jesus, sooner or later!" We all need to come to the Rock that is Christ, to be broken of our pride, selfishness, and sin. We will be broken on that rock, but we will be healed.

However, there is another group. They refuse to come to the Rock, they refuse to be broken in repentance. On this group, the Rock will fall. Instead of brokenness, they will be ground to dust. This is the judgment for all who refuse Christ. That's a scary thought. It makes the blood run cold.

Thankfully, we are in the first group. When you came to Christ, there was time of conviction, a time of brokenness. Through Christ's blood, now you have been healed! There may still be times of breaking in your future. God is always working on us, making us more Christlike. But the big decision has been made. You are His. Thank you, Jesus!

Let's Pray:
God, I know you don't want to bring judgment.
You gave your Son that we don't have to experience it.
Visit us in this hour that many will come to the Rock, Jesus!
In whose name we pray, Amen!

100 Days With Jesus

Day 75
Luke 21

COINS AND TOYS

As Jesus looked up, He saw the rich putting their gifts into the temple treasury. He also saw a poor widow put in two very small copper coins. "Truly I tell you," He said, "this poor widow has put in more than all the others." - Luke 21:1-3 (NIV)

Several years ago, our young family was involved in a six-week outreach in Mexico, and for part of that time we lived at an orphanage. Andrew was two-years old, and he loved to tell people that he was going to be "Tres in Septiembre!" While at the orphanage, Andrew naturally made friends with some of the kids.

Andrew was a happy kid, and he loved his toys. Even though we lived on a missionary's budget, Andrew had acres of toys back home. He had a special bag with his favorite toys he brought on the trip. These were his extra special toys. He was all set.

The children at the orphanage had very little in the way of the world's goods, but they were cheerful and loving. One day, a little boy who had made friends with Andrew gave him a red toy truck. It was small and beat up, and the wheels didn't turn very well, but it was a gift of gold.

This boy, who had nothing, gave one of the very few toys that he had. It was a gift of friendship and love, so it could not be returned. Mexicans are some of the most giving people on earth, and this young man was getting a good start at it.

A Journey Through The Gospels

So, picture the scene in our chapter today: fancy-dressed Pharisees and wealthy merchants opening bags of gold coins, dumping them into the treasury, making sure that they jangled them loudly so all could see and hear their philanthropy. Into this scenario Jesus says something shocking (just like He always did). After mentioning that the widow's gift was more than the others, He says why, "*For they all out of their surplus put into the offering; but she out of her poverty put in all that she had to live on*" (Luke 21:4).

We live in a land of plenty and a time of surplus. It can be easy to give out of that abundance. To be sure, some have had to walk down that widow's road. I've been amazed by how many people give sacrificially, being generous even when they have little. But very few of us have given as much as that widow. God may not call us to give every bit of our wealth at any time, but He will call us to sacrifice for others.

The widow gave all she had. So did Andrew's friend. Let's not cling too tightly to our coins and toys. Give them, and God will take care of the rest.

Let's Pray:
God, you have given me everything I need.
I have been blessed by the help of others.
Let me be your gift to someone else today.
In Jesus' name, Amen!

100 Days With Jesus

Day 76
Luke 22

MINISTERING ANGEL

Now an angel from heaven appeared to Him, strengthening Him. - Luke 22:43

Asralion peered over the banister of heaven. He was joined by the angelic multitudes as they watched the Son of God in the garden. Their hearts broke as they saw His agony. These angels had never known the pain that Jesus was going through. They had been in the glorious realm since the beginning. They had never known lack or emotional suffering, but they were servants of God, who is love. They knew love, and they knew that mighty love can cause a mighty breaking of the heart. Jesus was going through that now and their hearts broke for Him, but all they could do was watch.

Suddenly, Asralion heard his name being called. It was his chief, Michael. "You are being sent to minister to Jesus in His hour of greatest need," Michael said. Asralion did not feel adequate to the task of ministering to the Son of God, and the archangel knew that. "God will empower you with all grace as you go, my brother. Do not fear. He is with you." Asralion leapt through the gates of heaven and felt a new surge of power as he drew close to earth.

Jesus, in the garden, struggled mightily in prayer. Just as He felt His heart would explode with grief, He saw Asralion. The Savior

A Journey Through The Gospels

smiled through His pain. He knew this angelic friend and loved him. Asralion, with great reverence, laid his hand on Jesus, who felt new strength surge into His heart.

Have you ever wondered why God uses angels as His ministering agents? God could merely speak the answer we need into existence, but instead He sends angels. Sometimes the angels are even delayed because of the spiritual battle that rages all around them. Eventually they make it through and the purposes of God are achieved. Still, I wonder about it. Seems like an inefficient system, doesn't it?

Well, God isn't all about efficiency. He is all about relationship, however. God uses a being, an angel, who has thought and will and emotion, to accomplish His purposes. Sounds familiar; sounds like us. Almighty God doesn't need me or you, really, to accomplish what He wants. But He chooses relationship to be the agent through which the world is touched with His love.

God is going to use you to minister to someone today. You may feel inadequate to the task, but God will give you all the strength, wisdom and compassion you need. God knows you, and He knows you will represent Him well. And when you do, you will also minister to the heart of Jesus.

Let's Pray:
Lord, I pray that you will lead me to the one
who needs your touch today.
Let me reflect your glory in all I do and say.
In Jesus' name, Amen!

100 Days With Jesus

Day 77
Luke 23 .... *CARRYING JESUS' CROSS*

> *When they led Him away, they seized a man, Simon of Cyrene, coming in from the country, and placed on him the cross to carry behind Jesus.* - Luke 23:26

*V*ery little is known about Simon the Cyrene. The biblical accounts say he was in Jerusalem, and his sons Alexander and Rufus were with him. That's about all we know. Tradition says that he was a black man, Cyrene being in Africa. The only other thing we know is he carried Jesus' cross.

Our scripture today says Simon was seized and compelled by the soldiers to carry the cross. Was he unwilling and only did it by force? I'd like to think Simon felt compassion for Jesus. Perhaps he knelt near him as Jesus stumbled because he wanted to help. I hope that was the case.

Whatever his motivation, Simon carried Jesus' cross. I wonder what it felt like. Simon couldn't know that Jesus was about to bear a much greater burden when He was nailed to that cross. So, Simon trudges up the hill behind the stumbling figure of the Messiah. The cross is heavy, and the work is hard. His muscles ache and sweat drips from every pore. His arms are covered with splinters. At last, he reaches the top and lets go of the cross, lets go of the burden.

He then gets a front row seat to the crucifixion. Simon winces as

A Journey Through The Gospels

he can almost feel the cruel blows of the hammer. He wonders how anyone can endure such pain. Then he hears the even greater pain of the mocking crowd. He hears strange things from Jesus' mouth as He agonizes on the cross. The most powerful of which is *"Father forgive them."* He sees the sky darken. And finally, Jesus' lifeless body slumps forward. It is finished.

What did Simon do next? Did he try to forget it ever happened? Did he put it all out of his mind as he went to find his two sons? Again, we don't know. But we may have a hint. Remember, one of his sons was named Rufus. In Romans 16, Paul says, *"Greet Rufus, chosen of the Lord."* Was it the same Rufus? It's not clear, but tradition says that Rufus and Alexander, sons of Simon, became missionaries.

I'd like to think that's true. Their father carried Jesus' cross, but they did, too. It was a heart of love that caused Jesus to endure the cross. When we operate in that same heart of love, we carry His cross. Simon did … Rufus did … let us do that today.

Let's Pray:
Jesus, you endured the agony of the cross for the joy set before you, the joy of reuniting us with the Father. Help me to have that same motivation as I carry my cross today. In your name, Amen!

100 Days With Jesus

Day 78
Luke 24   *CLEOPAS AND JOE*

> They said to one another, "Were not our hearts burning within us while He was speaking to us on the road, while He was explaining the Scriptures to us?" - Luke 24:32

*O*ne of the amazing things about Jesus is the many attributes of God that He shows us in the Bible. He is the humble servant washing feet, and He is the Alpha and Omega of Revelation. He is the angry disrupter in the temple and the gentle rabbi whom the children love. He is the dying savior and the resurrected king.

One of my favorite pictures of Jesus in scripture is when He is walking with the two men on the road to Emmaus. One of them is named Cleopas. (The second one isn't named. We'll call him Joe.) Cleopas and Joe were just walking down the road discussing the events of the past few days, when a stranger joins them. It's Jesus, but they don't know it yet because He is hidden from their sight. But they love hearing what He is saying.

Cleopas and Joe have just witnessed the death of Jesus, so they need a little encouragement. As they walk, Jesus explains the prophecies concerning the Messiah. They begin to be hopeful, though they don't know why. Jesus exhorts them to have God's perspective on the situation.

A Journey Through The Gospels

Later, Jesus is revealed to them, but suddenly He disappears! Then they say our scripture verse today, *"were not our hearts burning!"* Their hearts were on fire with the truth that Jesus shared. And it was God's perspective that brought it home to them.

It's easy to make an application to any troubles you may face today. You see the dire circumstances all around you. You don't know how it will ever be better. But there is a God-perspective that you need to see. Don't be blind like Cleopas. Don't be slow to believe like Joe. But DO keep walking with Jesus and listening to His voice. Your heart will burn because you know what He is saying is true. His resurrection changes everything. You may be down in the dumps on Friday, but today is Sunday!

Let's Pray:
Heavenly Father, I love you.
Though I don't see my answer yet,
let me always see with your eyes.
Let me see things from your perspective.
I know that you are working in wonderful ways!
In Jesus' name, Amen!

100 Days With Jesus

Day 79
John 1   AN EMPTY CHAIR

And the Word became flesh, and dwelt among us, and we saw His glory, glory as of the only begotten from the Father, full of grace and truth. - John 1:14

The two angels reported for duty that morning as they had for 10,000 millennia. It was a bright morning, as it always was since their light was the light of God. No sun was needed in the heavenly realm. These angels served in the presence of Almighty God. As they approached the throne, they noticed that something was different. The throne at the right hand of the Father, the chair occupied by God the Son, was empty. Since eternity past He had occupied that place. "Where has He gone?" they wondered.

We understand that Jesus made a great sacrifice for us on the cross. He bore all the sin of mankind on his back. Can you imagine that? The sin of countless generations: my sin, your sin, Judas' sin, David's sin, every sin that has ever been committed can be forgiven because of Jesus' sacrifice.

We also know that Jesus made a great sacrifice in the wilderness, being tempted by the devil. He made a great sacrifice in prayer, in teaching, in persecution, and accusation by his enemies. He did it all because of His great love for me and you.

A Journey Through The Gospels

There is one other sacrifice we may not have considered. Since eternity past, Jesus had enjoyed a perfect, uninterrupted relationship with God the Father and God the Holy Spirit. What must that have been like? The Trinity had perfect joy, peace, and love for one another. Their unity was the very definition of oneness. They humbly served one another. All was bliss.

Suddenly, the Son is gone. His journey to earth caused Him to leave this trinitarian relationship in the fullness that He had known. Jesus still saw the Father. He still felt the Holy Spirit. He was still God. But now there was a veil of flesh between Jesus and the other two members of that fellowship. This was a huge sacrifice.

But for us it was glory! We see Him! We see the only begotten of the Father. We see the grace. We see the truth. He is the Truth! And Jesus, full of grace, has invited us into relationship with the Trinity.

We will never be God. But we do have fellowship with Him, even now. One day, we will be closer still, and we'll see that the Chair is no longer empty. Jesus is sitting at the right hand of the Father, full of grace and truth. I like to think that they are smiling.

Let's Pray:
Thank you Jesus for your sacrifice for me.
Thank you for your grace.
Thank you that I have fellowship with God
through you! In your name, Amen!

100 Days With Jesus

Day 80
John 2   *ZEAL FOR YOU*

> *And He made a scourge of cords, and drove them all out of the temple, with the sheep and the oxen; and He poured out the coins of the money changers and overturned their tables; and to those who were selling the doves He said, "Take these things away; stop making My Father's house a place of business." His disciples remembered that it was written, "Zeal for Your house will consume me." - John 2:15-17*

Jesus was happy to be heading to Jerusalem. He saw the crowds streaming in for Passover. A wild and passionate love was stirred in His heart for these who desired to know the Father, and yet, they were like sheep without a shepherd. He knew that soon they would be led astray by false teachers. The priests, scribes, Pharisees and Sadducees would bind them up with man's traditions! They would make each one twice a son of hell as themselves!

His passion was reaching a peak as He ascended to the temple. As He walked in, He hoped to see people at worship and at prayer. He hoped to see holiness and consecration. Instead He saw robbery and more. He saw lies! His anger — holy and righteous — was hot within Him!

He reached for some cords lying nearby...

It's hard to understand the gentle Savior wrecking the temple, isn't it? I think it's because we barely understand the depth of love that God has for us. God's heart was broken in the Garden when our

A Journey Through The Gospels

first parents, Adam and Eve, violated His command and relationship with Him was fractured. Our race had been cut off from the source of all peace and joy, the source of all meaning. God's creation, us, which He had called "Very good" was anything but good. We were in a pickle.

And we couldn't ever get ourselves out; God had to do it. Temple worship foreshadowed our ultimate restoration, when Jesus would institute a new covenant. God loved us so much that Jesus, His one and only Son, would sacrifice Himself for us (See John 3:16). We would finally be restored! As the Apostle John said, *See how great a love the Father has bestowed on us, that we would be called children of God!* (1 John 3:1)

Jesus cleansing the temple reflects God's zeal for relationship with His children. Anything that puts itself between Him and you, He wants out of the way. He would move a mountain for you! And He moved more than a mountain. The cross of Christ removed the veil. His sacrifice removed our punishment. Eventually, even the temple itself was removed.

There is nothing standing between you and God except willingness. Let's be willing today. It's going to be great!

Let's Pray:
Father, I turn my heart to you today.
Let's spend time together. I want to know you better.
I want to walk close to you, Lord.
In Jesus' name, Amen!

100 Days *With* Jesus

Day 81
John 3   *REVIVAL*

All who do evil hate the light and refuse to go near it for fear their sins will be exposed. -John 3:20, (NLT)

Lucius rode into town with an uneasy feeling. The dusty streets were deserted and he knew why. "That dratted travelin' preacher is in town. Everyone is at the church." Lucius didn't have much use for preachers. He dismounted and tied up Toby to the rail in front of the mercantile store, about a block from the church. He heard the singing and saw the lights, so he decided to head over. "It might be good for a lark," Lucius said to himself.

As he drew near to the church, he felt an urge, no, a compelling, to turn away. Yet he kept walking. Old Widow Barnes had been inviting him to come to church. He always found a way out of it. Now he wanted out, but he kept walking up the steps and through the doors. He slunk over to a seat in the last pew.

The preacher began. He spoke of sin! He spoke of violence, anger, drunkenness, and lust. His voice rose to a fever pitch. His face was red. On and on came the onslaught to Lucius' soul. He knew he was guilty of every sin! He knew he deserved judgment and the fires of hell! Lucius' blood ran cold in his veins. He wanted out, but there was no escape. He was nailed to that pew.

Just when he thought he could take no more, the preacher changed his tone. He read a scripture Lucius had never heard before, *"For*

A Journey Through The Gospels

God so loved the world, that he gave his only begotten Son, that whosoever believeth in Him should not perish, but have everlasting life" John 3:16 (KJV). "But I've been too bad," thought Lucius, "This can't be meant for me." The preacher had done his job too well. Condemnation flooded Lucius' heart.

Then the preacher read the next verse, *"For God sent not His Son into the world to condemn the world; but that the world through Him might be saved. He that believeth on Him is not condemned"* (John 3:17). A ray of hope pierced Lucius' spirit. Suddenly he understood God's grace and forgiveness.

An altar call was given. Lucius stood up and walked to the front with many others. A tear streamed down his rough cheek.

As Lucius rode Toby home that night, he felt fresh inside — new, like he had just been born! "I guess that's what that preacher means 'bout bein' born again," he said. Lucius smiled as he held his new Bible close.

―――――――――――

Our scripture today lets us know that the conviction of the Holy Spirit can be an uncomfortable thing. We want to hide our sins. But the love of God exposes them and forgives them. Praise God!

Let's Pray:
Heavenly Father, I thank You that your conviction leads us to repentance. Thank you for your grace. Let me never try to hide my sins from you. Help me to embrace your conviction and your forgiveness always.

100 Days With Jesus

Day 82
John 4

STARBUCKS GOSPEL

And Jacob's well was there. So Jesus, being wearied from His journey, was sitting thus by the well. It was about the sixth hour. There came a woman of Samaria to draw water. Jesus said to her, "Give Me a drink." - John 4:6-7

Mary walked into the coffee shop and placed her order. She got regular coffee, bypassing the caramel macchiatos and other "frou-frou" drinks. She also ordered a bran muffin as big as her head, well…almost. As she sat down, she just wanted a little time alone with God. She had her small Bible with her.

"What are ya reading?" a friendly old man asked, a table away. She had seen him at the shop before. He seemed safe enough to speak to, so she began to tell him a little about the gospel.

We have many interactions with strangers throughout each day. It may be on the bus, at the grocery store, or in the doctor's office waiting room. Most are polite but very brief. As Christians we want to be good ambassadors for Christ, so we try to treat people with respect and even let some of God's love shine through. A smile and a kind word can go a long way to brightening a person's day.

But deep within us there is a desire for something more. Can we make an impact for the kingdom of God through these brief conversations? Jesus thought so. He knew these daily conversations

A Journey Through The Gospels

were an open door for the love of God to be shared. He asked a brief question to the Samaritan woman. What resulted was simple but amazing.

Notice the conversation as you read John 4. Jesus started with a physical object (water). Pretty soon the talk became personal (call your husband). Then it became theological (where to worship). Finally, it became gospel: *"But an hour is coming, and now is, when the true worshipers will worship the Father in spirit and truth; for such people the Father seeks to be His worshipers"* (John 4:23).

Jesus' awesome love for this woman came shining through. He wanted her to be one of those 'Spirit and Truth' worshippers. He even declared himself as the Messiah to her! She was so overcome by what Jesus had shared with her, she just had to tell others (Come, see!). She went from a woman in a despised minority to a proclaimer of the Christ.

All from a conversation about water.

You will meet *someone* today. What will you leave with them?

Let's Pray:
Father, let me be a kind and gracious witness for you today. Help me to spread your love to every dark corner. In Jesus' name, Amen!

100 Days With Jesus

Day 83
John 5

WILD MEN FOR GOD

He was the lamp that was burning and was shining and you were willing to rejoice for a while in His light. - John 5:35

*I*magine you are a first-century Jew. You live in the land of your ancestors, in the land of promise, on the homestead of your fathers, but things are not all right.

The Promised Land is ruled by the Romans. These pagans have invaded and occupy the ground promised to Abraham, and to you! They are brutal worshippers of false gods. You know it was the failures of your ancestors that led to this present situation. You know that God wants clean hands and a pure heart, and you know those who lived in the time of the kings did not have those qualities. You want your generation to be better.

You have spiritual leaders: priests, scribes, Pharisees and Sadducees. But they are either in league with the Romans or are just interested in fighting one another. Finally, there are the zealots. You like their passion for Israel, but you know something is off. All they want to do is kill Romans.

So, you ask yourself: *Where is God in all this*? Suddenly a strange man appears; he is a wild man preaching in the wilderness. His words have the ring of truth and the power of God in them. You begin to follow this Baptist. You wonder: Is this the Messiah?

A Journey Through The Gospels

But no. Even John the Baptist says he is not the Christ. But he speaks of another to come soon. You keep your eyes peeled. One day you hear about a strange new prophet in the land. Not just a preacher, but a miracle-worker! You are hopeful, but you've been disappointed by "holy men" before. Still, you go to see this Jesus of Nazareth. His words don't just speak of God's power as John's did, but they are FILLED with power. You start to follow Him closely. Even John tells you to go to Him. Finally, you hear Jesus say these words, *"But the testimony which I have is greater than the testimony of John; for the works which the Father has given Me to accomplish — the very works that I do — testify about Me, that the Father has sent Me"* (John 5:36).

That settles it. You follow Jesus through thick and thin. Eventually, you understand. Jesus did not come to get rid of Romans. He came to defeat a greater enemy. He came to save your soul from sin. You follow Him through betrayal, beating, death, burial, and resurrection.

He tells you to go into all the world and make disciples. Suddenly, there is a new wild man on the edge of town proclaiming the love of God.

It's you.

Let's Pray:
Jesus, thank you for choosing me and saving me.
Give me your heart for what really matters.
Help me to share your love with others today.
In your name, Amen!

100 Days With Jesus

Day 84
John 6

YOU DA MONSTER

As a result of this many of His disciples withdrew and were not walking with Him anymore. - John 6:66

I don't know if you ever watched some of the old monster movies from the 1950's and 60's. They were cheesy, with bad acting and bad sets, but they had a great monster: *Godzilla!* I don't know where he came from; he would just sort of walk out of the sea and start mashing up the city. Pretty soon the army would be called out to stop him. He wasn't too fast, speed was not one of Godzilla's super-powers, but he was strong and seemingly unaffected by anything the army threw at him. Guns, bazookas, tanks and missiles did not affect Godzilla. That was his scariest quality; He could not be stopped. He would just plod along smashing another building as he went, plod, plod, plod.

In our text today, Jesus sees many of his disciples leave. How this must have saddened his heart! He had just finished laying out the difficult terms of what it meant to be one of His disciples. Some people, perhaps most people, could not bear it.

Dejectedly, Jesus turns to his closest disciples and asks, *"You do not want to go away also, do you?"* (John 6:67a). To read this breaks my heart. I'm sure God's heart was broken, too, at the many who had

A Journey Through The Gospels

gone away. Peter responds, and his words ring down the corridors of history to us today, *"Lord, to whom shall we go? You have words of eternal life."* No, they would not be leaving.

Being a disciple of Christ is a glorious thing, but also a difficult one. It is not a life of ease. The old hymn, *Amazing Grace* said it well in verse three, *"Through many dangers, toils, and snares I have already come."* There will be many pitfalls as you follow after Jesus. And your enemy will try to send fiery missiles at you to try to trip you up or make you turn away. We've all known people who started well on the Christian journey and then left the path.

You know what I think? I think we all need to be a little bit more like Godzilla. Just keep plodding along in Christ, moving forward in faith, no matter what the enemy throws at us. One more thing about those cheesy movies. Pretty soon Godzilla caught up to the army and mashed them! Then everyone started running away. How great a spiritual principle is that! As you plod ahead in the power of Christ, your enemies will flee.

We are in this race for the long haul. Don't quit before the finish line. You da monster!

Let's Pray:
God, sometimes I feel like giving up
but I know you want me to keep moving.
Give me your strength today and your faith by which
I can extinguish the fiery missiles of the enemy.
In Jesus' name, Amen!

100 Days With Jesus

Day 85
John 7

HONEY FROM THE ROCK

"Do not judge according to appearance, but judge with righteous judgment."
- John 7:24

Reverend Lang walked into the sanctuary and heartily greeted his fellow pastors. The regional pastor's conference was about to get underway, and he was really looking forward to it. He loved these times of refreshing from the great men of God. He enjoyed hearing from the learned doctors of the faith.

As he shook hands with Pastor Barkley from Smithville, he noticed a disheveled man in second-hand clothes on the platform. "Who is that character?" he asked his friend, thinking that the man was in the wrong place. "That's tonight's speaker," said Pastor Barkley, and he smiled as he said it.

Reverend Lang was disappointed. How was he going to learn from this rough character in the tattered coat? Where were the theologians he loved to hear? Ah well, there was nothing else to do but sit and listen.

The songs ended and the speaker was introduced. He was a farmer from the local community, but as he shared the Word of God, the Holy Spirit descended, anointing his words with the divine presence. Pastor Lang felt awash in the love of God. He repented of his earlier

A Journey Through The Gospels

view of the man and thought, "He gave us honey from the rock tonight!"

After the service, he went up to the man and asked, "Sir, where did you get that message?" The farmer shared his practice of reading just two lines from the Bible in the morning and then walking the lane at his farm, meditating on that scripture. God would give him fresh revelation as he did.

The people in Jesus' time were constantly judging Him by sight. "He is uneducated; He is from that backwater Galilee; He heals on the Sabbath; He eats with sinners; He has a demon!" They just couldn't get over His appearance. Jesus didn't look or act like their concept of how a messiah should look or act. They missed the blessing of God by their unrighteous judgment.

We're all used to judging by sight; we've done it all our lives. We are impressed by clothes, cars, degrees, and titles. God has a different view. He is looking for a heart after Him!

Let's Pray:
God let me always be open to the Word of God
no matter who the messenger is. Let me not judge
a book by its cover, but let me see with your eyes.
In Jesus' name, Amen!

PS: The story above about the farmer is true. I heard it from an old-time preacher from Scotland, Campbell McAlpine. Many thanks to him for sharing it!

100 Days With Jesus

Day 86
John 8 *Truth Keys*

> *So Jesus said to the Jews who had believed Him, "If you abide in My word, you are truly My disciples, and you will know the truth, and the truth will set you free."* - John 8:31-32 (ESV)

I recently received a message from my car. (What a brave new world we live in!) The message was in the middle of my dashboard, and it said "Change Key Battery." Now first off, my car hasn't got a key, it has a key fob. "Fob" is not a word that I had much occasion to use before buying this car, but I use the word all the time now. "Hey, honey. Where's my fob?" See, my vocabulary is expanding.

Anyhoo... I sort of knew that my key fob had a battery, but I never thought about replacing it. Now I had to replace it. I couldn't figure out how to do it, as hard as I tried. So I watched a YouTube video on it before I broke something. It turns out that my fob has a hidden key. I knew that already, because the dealer explained it. However, a new thought occurred to me. The key would open my door if my fob had a dead battery, but it wouldn't start my car. So, if I was stranded I could get in and sit down in my car to heart's content, but I couldn't go anywhere! What gives?

Well, it turns out my little fob has even bigger secrets! There is a little chip inside the fob that works even without a battery. You

A Journey Through The Gospels

just put it close to the "Start" button, and then push the button. Your car recognizes the chip, and you may now drive away, dead fob, hidden key, and all.

My key fob seems to be prepared for every eventuality. But what about me and my spiritual life? Am I prepared for every spiritual eventuality? No, the key fob won't pray for me… not yet anyway! However, there is a way we can be prepared; a way to have a hidden spiritual reserve set aside in my heart and mind. It's called *abiding*.

In our text, Jesus calls His hearers to abide in His word. This abiding is what marks us as Jesus' disciples. And it does much more. It gives us something called *truth*. Contrary to popular opinion, truth is not one thing to me and something else to you. Truth is truth, and that truth is found in Jesus' words. The truth found there is transformative.

Truth makes me what I am not. I am dead; it makes me alive. I am weak; it makes me strong. I am foolish, and it makes me wise. I am bound and it makes me free.

Are you abiding in Christ's words today? If you find yourself far off, now is the time to take a look at His book. Now is the time to abide.

Let's Pray:
Jesus, I have your words with me at all times.
Help me to abide in them.
Make me free today, O Lord!
In your name I pray, Amen!

100 Days With Jesus

Day 87
John 9 —— **THE PROOF**

And said to him, "Go, wash in the pool of Siloam" (which is translated, Sent). So he went away and washed, and came back seeing. - John 9:7

Ezra stood with his mouth wide open! How could this young man see? He had known him since they were both children. He knew he was born blind. As a member of the Sanhedrin, Ezra knew that he could not accept Jesus' teaching. After all, He was an untrained carpenter from Galilee. He could not be a prophet, much less the Messiah.

Ezra finally closed his mouth and thought hard. Here was his blind boyhood friend seeing things for the first time. Jesus had just performed an incredible miracle. That could not be denied. But then, He had done it on the Sabbath: Jesus had worked on the Sabbath. How could He be a prophet? As the youngest member of the priestly class, Ezra felt that he should keep silent. That may have been a good thing, because the elders were getting nowhere asking his friend questions. In fact, they were getting into deeper trouble. His friend had an answer for everything.

Ezra thought to himself, "Who is this Jesus, though?"

As we read John 9, we see a man healed of blindness. Then we have the most intense questioning of a miracle found anywhere in

A Journey Through The Gospels

the New Testament. The formerly blind man is grilled by the Pharisees, but he has an answer for their every question. They try to revile Jesus and question the blind man's credentials (John 9: 9,18). They even harangue his parents, who should be overjoyed for their son, but who chicken out when questioned (John 9:21).

Enduring all this interrogation, the man finally reaches the pinnacle of logic. After they call Jesus a sinner, he testifies to the truth of Jesus: *He then answered, "Whether He is a sinner, I do not know; one thing I do know, that though I was blind, now I see"* (John 9: 25).

I love this guy!

There is an old saying, "The proof of the pudding is in the tasting." It means that no matter what you or I say or think, proof by its very definition, must be proven. The man's healing is proof of who Jesus is, no matter what the Pharisees say. They should have recognized it, but they were the ones who were truly blind.

Ezra, on the edge of the crowd, saw his friend speaking to Jesus. Now he saw him bowing before Him. Jesus did not rebuke him. "Perhaps the elders are wrong," he said to himself. "I think I'll talk to my friend Nicodemus about this."

Let's Pray:
Jesus, let me always see you for who you really are.
Let me be a speaker of truth like the man born blind.
Heal me, and I will tell of your goodness!
In your name, Amen!

100 Days With Jesus

Day 88
John 10 — HIS VOICE

> *I am the good shepherd, and I know My own and My own know Me.*
> *- John 10:14*

*I*t was a nice summer's day right after church several years ago. I was standing outside taking in the sun. People were milling around and visiting, though most were moving inexorably to their cars for the drive home. Suddenly, I saw Michael.

Michael was the little brother of my good friend Carmine. They were from a big Italian family, and even though Carmine was in his twenties, Michael was only about 4 years old. Michael walked up to me without really looking at me. He grabbed a hold of my hand and then began to say, "Carmine, I..." Suddenly he looked up and saw that I was not his big brother! He quickly removed his hand from mine and ran off, I suppose to find someone who wasn't impersonating Carmine.

Jesus refers to himself as the Good Shepherd. Since the Israelites of his day were surrounded by shepherds and surrounded by sheep, they could easily identify with the analogy. Shepherds cared for their sheep by working long hours with them. The sheep become comfortable with their shepherd. They knew him and knew how well he took care of them. Most important of all, they knew his voice.

A Journey Through The Gospels

The shepherd would sing aloud or play a harp as he sat among the sheep. They would be comforted by his soothing voice. If he cried out, they knew that danger was near and would move closer to him and away from harm. Wolves tried to sneak up on the sheep, but a good shepherd could chase them away. If a sheep got foolish (not an uncommon occurrence) and strayed, that sheep was in great danger.

Sheep could even get fooled. Little Michael thought I was his brother because Carmine and I were both tall and skinny. Michael saw long legs in blue jeans and figured he had the right person. Upon closer examination, he realized his error. How easily a sheep might make such an error and it might be too late.

When we are in the sheepfold with Christ, we get to know Him. We know His voice, and He tells us that we will not follow another. But if we stray from Him, we are in danger. There are "wolves in sheep's clothing" all about.

Today, listen and look. Jesus is speaking to us, and He wants us to follow Him. Don't stray from Him or from His flock.

Let's Pray:
Jesus, thank you for being my Good Shepherd.
Help me to always hear your voice clearly.
If I stray, rescue me, Lord!
In your name I pray, Amen!

100 Days With Jesus

Day 89
John 11 — LORD OF THE NOW

So Jesus then said to them plainly, "Lazarus is dead." - John 11:14

The disciples didn't really understand. Martha didn't understand. Even her sister, beloved Mary, didn't comprehend the full extent of who He was. The priests didn't want to understand.

It was dear Martha, bold and forthright who got it out of Him. She questioned him about why He hadn't come sooner. He told her that Lazarus would rise. She was slowly getting it, but not quite yet, *Martha said to Him, "I know that he will rise again in the resurrection on the last day"* (John 11:24). This wasn't wrong, of course. There would be a final resurrection of the righteous. But that was far off. Lazarus needed a miracle now.

Jesus declares to Martha some of the most powerful words ever spoken, *"I am the resurrection and the life; he who believes in Me will live even if he dies, and everyone who lives and believes in Me will never die. Do you believe this?"* (John 11: 25-26)

Martha says that she does, and hope begins to rise in her heart. Practical and hardworking, Martha is about to get a lesson in what the power of God is really like. It is not just a power for a far-off

A Journey Through The Gospels

day, though it is that. No. The power is for right now. Jesus is Lord of the Now!

Jesus begins to walk to the tomb. Mary falls at His feet. Those gathered begin to wonder aloud about His claims.

Jesus wept.

Fully God and fully human, Jesus allows His humanity full expression. He wept, aloud and long. How else would everyone have seen it? Perhaps He wept at the group's hardness of heart, but it was more than that. Jesus wept because that's what human beings do when a loved one dies.

But the Lord of the Now had more to do than weep. The stone was removed, and He spoke the words, *"Lazarus, come forth!"* And he came! No longer weeping, Jesus greeted His friend with a knowing glance, almost as if to say, "Sorry to have to bring you back, old friend, but this group needs to know a few things." Lazarus was cool with it.

From that day forward, all those who loved Jesus walked with a new understanding. Jesus is Lord. He is Lord of the Now.

Let's Pray:
Jesus, I know my salvation is sure.
I know I will rise again in the resurrection.
But I need your power today, Lord.
Help me trust in you now.
In your name, Amen!

100 Days With Jesus

Day 90
John 12 — TESTIMONY

> *The large crowd of the Jews then learned that He was there; and they came, not for Jesus' sake only, but that they might also see Lazarus, whom He raised from the dead. Because on account of him many of the Jews were going away and were believing in Jesus.* - John 12:9,11

Lazarus made his way down the alleyway and out into the main thoroughfare. It was beginning to happen again. People were watching him. They were standing in little groups and gawking; occasionally a whispered comment passed between them. Lazarus was a celebrity in his hometown. Three weeks ago, he was dead. Now he was alive, raised by Jesus! He let that sink in once again.

Lazarus had seen the portals of heaven and heard the praise of the archangel ascending to the throne. Now he was back to the sounds of the city. Earth would never hold his affection again.

Lazarus knew he was meant to be more than a curiosity. He knew that he was not given a glimpse of heaven for his own satisfaction. He was to be a witness! As the crowd began to form around him, Lazarus turned and began to preach the gospel of the kingdom to them. He began to testify of Jesus the Messiah. Many believed.

As we read in our text today, the testimony of Lazarus was leading many to faith in Christ. The Bible never even says that Lazarus said anything, but I'm sure that he did. How could he remain silent!

A Journey Through The Gospels

Look at who else was sharing. *"So, the people who were with Him when He called Lazarus out of the tomb and raised him from the dead, continued to testify about Him"* (John 12: 17). God's wonders are never for our own personal fulfillment alone. We are called to give testimony of His miracles. What we have seen Him do helps us declare His Lordship.

Not everyone will be happy about that. The Jewish religious leaders, who had been plotting to murder Jesus, now wanted to kill Lazarus because people were believing in Jesus because of him (John 12: 10). Think of that! They wanted to kill a man who had already been dead. How's that working for you, Caiaphas?

As with Lazarus, we are witnesses of Christ's power. He will bring someone to you who needs to know Him. Maybe today. Don't fear those who would silence you. Just open your mouth and God will fill it.

"It will lead to an opportunity for your testimony" (Luke 21:13).

Let's Pray:
*Heavenly Father, thank you for the miracles
you have done for me. Give me
the opportunity and boldness to speak for you
to anyone you bring in my path.
I trust in you! In Jesus' name, Amen.*

100 Days With Jesus

Day 91
John 13 — ***THE MARK OF A CHRISTIAN***

A new commandment I give to you, that you love one another, even as I have loved you, that you also love one another. - John 13:34

Growing up, I attended a church that came from the holiness tradition. It was a good church with good people, but there was a lot of emphasis on external behaviors. The church's charter had some rules like "don't dance, don't go to movies, and don't read the newspaper on Sundays." (I'm not making this up.) These were the marks of someone who was really following the Lord, I guess. Obviously, no good Christian would smoke or drink or cuss. We don't want to look like the world. We need to be above reproach!

Hey, I'm not saying you should smoke or drink or cuss. We need to live lives that glorify God. All I'm saying is Jesus has a higher and better distinguishing mark for his followers, *"Love one another."*

The Book of John is unique in that it spends its second half concentrating on just one week of Jesus' life, the week leading up to His crucifixion. Jesus begins by celebrating the Passover with His disciples. He hasn't got much time left with them, so He tells and shows them some very important things.

In John 13, Jesus begins demonstrating the role of a servant by washing the disciples' feet. It was such a dirty job that Jesus had to take off His robe to keep it from getting soiled. He then went to

A Journey Through The Gospels

each person one-by-one and washed them. What must have it been like when He washed Judas' feet? Serving the one He knew would soon betray Him! Perhaps it was also a last chance for Judas to repent.

After Judas leaves to betray Him, the Savior tells the remaining disciples quite plainly what it means to follow Him. He tells them that the mark of a Christian is love. He starts with our opening verse today and then makes it even clearer, *"By this all men will know that you are My disciples, if you have love for one another"* (John 13:35).

Love is a verb. It is an action word. Love means that we are doing something to show our love to a person. Do you know what the opposite of love is? I'll bet you'd say *hate*. Not really. The opposite of love is *apathy*. The opposite of love is not caring for your brother or sister.

There is an old saying: "If being a Christian was illegal, would there be enough evidence to convict you?" If you love your brothers and sisters, you will be displaying all the evidence that anyone needs to know that you are truly a follower of Christ.

Love one another and you will be guilty of the true mark of a Christian!

Let's Pray:
Jesus, help me to know you and love you.
Help me to love others as you love me. Show me
someone who needs love today. Show me how
to love them. In your name I pray, Amen!

100 Days With Jesus

Day 92
John 14 — HIS PLACE

> *In My Father's house are many dwelling places; if it were not so, I would have told you; for I go to prepare a place for you.* - John 14:2

My family has a cabin in northern Pennsylvania and I've been going there my entire life. It's a little place, kind of dumpy, made with second-hand materials that my steelworker grandfather could economically purchase. It will not be on the cover of any *Home and Garden* magazines anytime soon. But it's a great place.

The cabin has always been a refuge to me. It's quiet; there is no internet, no broadcast TV, and usually no cell phone signal. It is a place to relax and recharge. There are a lot of outdoor activities to do nearby, but you don't have to do any of them. You can just sit by the campfire if that's all you want to do. It's Heaven to me. I hope you have a similar retreat in your life.

Jesus says in our text today, He goes to prepare a place for us. That's an exciting prospect! Think of your favorite place on the earth, ever. Is it the beach, your grandma's kitchen, or your mother's lap? Is it your old bedroom, or a treehouse you and your brother built out back? I'm willing to wager that each of us have such a place in mind.

A Journey Through The Gospels

We loved that place because we felt secure. We could be our true self. There were no duties asked of us. We could reside confidently in that setting because it was full of grace. We could even reach our potential through encouragement rather than demands.

A place of refuge speaks to a deep longing in us. There is a place our heart cries out for, a place beyond this world. It is our true home. Jesus prepares such a place for us.

But a home is not just a house. The cabin wouldn't be a refuge if my wife wasn't there. My relationship with Jean is an integral part of any refuge. It's the same with our heavenly home. It is a relationship we seek more than a building.

Jesus is seeking it, too. In anticipation of it, He says in the very next verse, *"And if I go and prepare a place for you, I will come back and take you to be with me that you also may be where I am"* (John 14:3, NIV).

We are not going to love Heaven because it has great draperies or a gourmet kitchen. We will love it because He will be there. Jesus is our ultimate refuge.

Let's Pray:
Lord, let me always remember that
you are my final destination. In you I find
true and lasting peace. Amen!

100 Days With Jesus

Day 93
John 15 — *NO BONFIRES IN JESUS' BACKYARD!*

"I am the true vine, and My Father is the vinedresser. Every branch in Me that does not bear fruit, He takes away; and every branch that bears fruit, He prunes it so that it may bear more fruit." - John 15:1-2

Jean and I have had quite a battle with vines invading the evergreen trees in our backyard. You may not see them at a quick glance, but they are there, filling the upper branches. After we moved in seven years ago, we sought out the source of the vines. It was a massive root about 4 inches in diameter! We cut it, and we thought our problems were over. Not so.

Every year the vines try to come back. There are new shoots all the time. We just cut a root last week, and you can see the results of our "death blow" in the treetops. Brown vines everywhere. We love that brown color. It means we're winning!

Of course, not all vines are bad. When I was growing up, my grandmother had grape vines in her backyard. It was great to get the sweet grapes right off the vine. They were so tasty! I feel the same way about tomatoes. Nothing better.

Our scripture today speaks of the very best type of vine, a spiritual one. Jesus calls himself the "true vine." Then suddenly, He speaks of a scary prospect. The branches of the vine that don't produce fruit will be cut off and thrown into the fire. Just in case the disciples didn't get the analogy, He tells them they are the branches.

A Journey Through The Gospels

And we are, too. I sure don't want to be one of those branches cut and tossed!

Thankfully, Jesus tells us how we can avoid that, *"Abide in Me, and I in you. As the branch cannot bear fruit of itself unless it abides in the vine, so neither can you unless you abide in Me"* (John 15:4). I love this verse because it's clear that Jesus wants us to succeed. He is not looking to have a branch bonfire anytime soon.

But how do we abide in Him? It's by keeping His commandments, which is something we want to do anyway. It is by abiding in His love and the Father's love. *"You will abide in My love; just as I have kept My Father's commandments and abide in His love"* (John 15: 10b).

Jesus also promised a great prize when we abide, *"These things I have spoken to you so that My joy may be in you, and that your joy may be made full"* (John 15:11).

There you have it. When you and I abide, we have a connection to the root, Jesus, who gives us fullness of joy. We won't be an annoying backyard vine up a tree. We will be a vine bearing beautiful fruit to His glory!

Let's pray:
Father, abiding and fruit are to be the
center of my Christian life. Many times,
I lose sight of my real purpose.
Today, let me abide in your love!
In Christ's name, Amen!

100 Days With Jesus

Day 94
John 16 —— **FATHER'S DAY**

> *'In that day you will ask in My name, and I do not say to you that I will request of the Father on your behalf; for the Father Himself loves you.'*
> - John 16:26-27a (ESV)

Jimmy could hear the car pull into the driveway. A shock of cold fear ran through his body as he thought of his father coming up the stairs. He was late from work which, as even young Jimmy knew, meant that his dad had stopped at the bar on the way home. Soon the yelling would start. His mother got the worst of it, but Jimmy took a lot of abuse, too. Jimmy just hoped no one would get hit.

Even at age eight, Jimmy knew that it didn't have to be like this. He loved it on an occasional Saturday morning when Dad would take him fishing. Sometimes they would go to a baseball game together. His dad was a good man then. Jimmy loved those days.

Today wasn't one of those days. He heard his father's loud voice and slurred speech downstairs, and he shivered.

What is that picture conjured in your mind when you hear the word *Father*? For many of us, I hope most of us, we imagine a loving, strong, and playful person; one who could make us laugh with his jokes or silly antics. Maybe you think of the times together when

A Journey Through The Gospels

he taught you how to fix your bike or swing a hammer. Maybe it was just sitting on his lap as you watched your favorite TV program. Or do you think of the picture each day as he gave your mom a hug and kiss?

These are the pictures God wants us to see when we think of Him. In our text today, Jesus says an amazing thing. He tells the disciples that God Himself, the eternal Father and Creator, loves them just like Jesus does.

When God calls Himself our Father, He is not using a mere analogy. God is our Father! Part of growth in Christ is that we begin to get an accurate picture of our heavenly Father. Jesus revealed Him to us, and the Holy Spirit is leading us into all truth about Him.

God intended our earthly fathers to reflect the image of our heavenly Father to us. Many of them did a very good job of that, including my own father. Sadly, many others hear the word "Father" and the image is of an abusive, neglectful, or absent man. If that is you, then know God is at work in you, reshaping the image of what a wonderful Father He is.

Let's Pray:
Father, thank you for creating me and saving me.
Thank you for revealing your heart to me.
Help me see you how you really are.
In Jesus' name, Amen!

100 Days With Jesus

Day 95
John 17 *YOU'RE IN THE BIBLE*

"My prayer is not for them alone. I pray also for those who will believe in Me through their message." - John 17:20 (NIV)

Andrew told it to Peter. Peter told the 3,000. Philip told it to the Ethiopian eunuch, and he told it to Ethiopia. The disciples told it to Thomas. Thomas told India. Jesus told Paul in a vision. Paul told Festus and Agrippa and Timothy and Asia, Athens, Rome, and Spain. And he told Caesar's household.

Count Zinzendorf told the Moravians, who told John and Charles Wesley. John preached it 40,000 times. Charles, his brother, wrote it in over 6,500 hymns, which have been sung for over 250 years. (Hmmm... if one of Charles' hymns was sung in one church every Sunday and there are hundreds of thousands of churches, so that's 100,000 hymns x 250 years x 52 Sundays/year = a bunch of times it was shared!)

Edward Kimbell told it to DL Moody, who shared it with millions of people. Mordecai Ham shared it with Billy Graham, who told it to more people than anyone has ever talked to in the history of the world. JRR Tolkien, the author of *The Lord of the Rings*, told it to CS Lewis, the author of the *Chronicles of Narnia*. CS Lewis explained it to millions of others in books and on the radio. And... someone shared it with you. It is the good news of the Gospel.

A Journey Through The Gospels

Jesus, when He prayed in the week leading up to His crucifixion, prayed for His current disciples first. Then He prayed for all those who would believe in Him because of their word. That, down through many long generations, is me and you.

Jesus prayed for you! And listen to what he prayed for you: *"that all of them may be one, Father, just as You are in Me and I am in You. May they also be in Us so that the world may believe that You have sent Me. I have given them the glory that You gave Me, that they may be one as We are one — I in them and You in Me — so that they may be brought to complete unity. Then the world will know that You sent Me and have loved them even as You have loved Me"* (John 17:21-23 NIV).

When we walk in love and unity, the world knows who Jesus is because they see His glory in us. Someone shared that glory with you. Jesus prayed for them to do it because He cares for you. He wanted to get you the good news.

Now it's your turn. With whom will you share the good news? Perhaps it's the next DL Moody.

The world is waiting.

Let's pray:
Father, I thank you for that person who brought the gospel to me. I thank you that I have the privilege of knowing you and being your child. Help me to shine your glory on someone today! In Jesus' name, Amen!

100 Days With Jesus

Day 96
John 18   *I AM HE*

> *"Whom do you seek?" They answered Him, "Jesus the Nazarene." He said to them, "I am He." And Judas also, who was betraying Him, was standing with them. So when He said to them, "I am He," they drew back and fell to the ground. - John 18:4b-6*

Marcus was stirred out of his sleep, and he wasn't too happy about it. Something big was finally happening though, and he didn't want to miss it. He was tired of these Jews and their ways. Here he was, a Roman soldier, doing their dirty work tonight. But his curiosity about this false prophet, this Jesus, had gotten the better of him. Who was this man the Jewish leaders feared and hated so much?

Marcus and the other men approached the garden with the Pharisees and a strange man at the front. Judas was his name, and he claimed to know Jesus' hiding place. Wanting to get a good look at Jesus, Marcus worked his way to the front of the men. He heard the commander say they were looking for Jesus. He heard Jesus' answer, "I Am He." And that was the last thing he remembered.

Suddenly Marcus found himself flat on his back. He got up a bit groggy and saw that all of them were in the same situation. He didn't know what happened, but he knew some power had come out of Jesus. His training kicked in and he moved to arrest the prophet. But strange new thoughts were running through his mind.

A Journey Through The Gospels

Jesus responded to the question of *who the soldiers sought* with an interesting phrase, *"I am He."* The Apostle John in recording this scene uses the Greek phrase *ego eimi*, which literally means *I am*. Sound familiar? Jesus was using the title God had reserved for Himself. It was the title Moses heard from the burning bush. Jesus is making a statement.

But words are cheap. Results are what matters. When Jesus says, "I am," the soldiers stumble backward and fall to the ground. The power of this one truth of who Jesus really is, is so earth-shattering that they cannot stand up under the weight of it.

Jesus is still taken prisoner. He is still going to die on the cross. But those who heard and those who fell will never forget the power of His words. I hope that several got to experience the power of His resurrection.

Christ lives in you. The Holy Spirit empowers you. This power is available to you. But greater still is that you now have a relationship with the source of that power. Jesus is the great I Am!

Let's Pray:
Heavenly Father, I feel so weak at times.
Let me always remember that the life of Christ
dwells in me. Help me to see your power today.
In Jesus' name, Amen.

100 Days With Jesus

Day 97
John 19   WILLINGLY

"It is finished!" - John 19:30

Nailed To The Cross

"There was One who was willing to die in my stead,
That a soul so unworthy might live,
And the path to the cross He was willing to tread,
All the sins of my life to forgive.

They are nailed to the cross,
They are nailed to the cross,
O how much He was willing to bear!
With what anguish and loss,
Jesus went to the cross!
But He carried my sins with Him there."

-Carrie Ellis Breck

Jesus left the joys of heaven to come to earth and experience the life of man. He taught us how to live. He performed miracles, and He demonstrated the heart of a servant. He told us to love our enemies. And He showed us the love of the Father.

And yet all of this was not the main reason Jesus came. John 19 shows us that reason: He came to die. He came to bear the penalty of sin as

A Journey Through The Gospels

Paul says, "*Having canceled out the certificate of debt consisting of decrees against us, which was hostile to us; and He has taken it out of the way, having nailed it to the cross*" (Colossians 2:14).

And yet it was Jesus Himself who was nailed to the cross. He carried the penalty of my sin and yours. He did it willingly. As He said in John 10:18, *"No one takes My life from Me. I give it up willingly! I have the power to give it up and the power to receive it back again, just as my Father commanded Me to do"* (CEV).

How easily Jesus could have stopped the soldiers. He could have deposed Pilate and Herod. He could have called on 10,000 legions of angels and defeated the power of the Roman Empire. He could have set up His kingdom.

But we would still be dead in our sins. Instead, He went to the cross and died, and said, "*It Is Finished!*"

Let's Pray:
*Jesus, I thank you for your love,
which took away my sin.
Thank you for your sacrifice for me.
Praise your holy name!*

100 Days With Jesus

Day 98
John 20 — **WRITTEN FOR US**

But these have been written so that you may believe that Jesus is the Christ, the Son of God; and that believing you may have life in His name. - John 20:31

John sat alone in his chamber staring out the window, watching the breakers crash against the rocks. His accommodations in Ephesus were spare, but comfortable enough.

The aged apostle rolled out the clean piece of parchment that sat on the table in front of him. He stretched his gnarled hands to loosen them up for writing. Before he dipped his pen though, he thought and prayed. "Why now?" he wondered aloud. Matthew, Mark, and Luke had written their gospels years ago. They were well known to those of the Way. John felt inadequate to the task. "It has been fifty long years since those days," he said to himself. But as he grasped for the quill, he felt the glow of the Holy Spirit on him. "I will teach you what to write," the third Person of the Trinity said. "You will glorify Jesus with your pen, and many will come to know the Savior through your gospel. Trust in Me as you write. I will bring everything needful to your memory."

John began to write, haltingly at first, but then the words began to flow as if directly from heaven, *"In the beginning was the Word, and the Word was with God, and the Word was God."*

A Journey Through The Gospels

God wanted to communicate His love to us. He wanted it to last beyond the spoken word. So, He inspired 40 writers over 1,500 years to write the words that we now know as the Bible. Most important of all the words of the Bible are the four books we call the gospels: Matthew, Mark, Luke and John. These tell us of Jesus and how we may be saved through Him.

How wonderful that we have the written Word of God that we can hold in our hands, carry with us, and read every day! Though at times it has been outlawed and suppressed, even by people who called themselves Christians, the Bible is still with us. The love of God is not lost.

Cherish your Bible. Many people went through great difficulty to get it to you. Some even lost their lives. But you have the Word of God in your hands through their sacrifice.

Let's Pray:
Heavenly Father, thank you for giving me your words.
Thank you for the comfort and conviction that they bring.
Let your Word change me today!
In Jesus' name, Amen!

100 Days With Jesus

Day 99
John 21

Do You Love Me?

So when they had finished breakfast, Jesus said to Simon Peter, "Simon, son of John, do you love Me more than these?" He said to Him, "Yes, Lord; You know that I love You." - John 21:15a

The disciples are fishing in a post-resurrection world. They have seen Jesus, but He isn't there now. Suddenly, they see a man on the shore, and He tells them where to catch a big bunch of fish. Great! But then this odd thing happens.

Therefore that disciple whom Jesus loved said to Peter, "It is the Lord." So when Simon Peter heard that it was the Lord, he put his outer garment on (for he was stripped for work), and threw himself into the sea" (John 21:7).

Don't you wonder what a fully-clothed Peter was thinking about as he was bobbing up and down in the sea? Why did he throw himself in the water? He probably didn't want to face Jesus again. He had betrayed Him, and though I'm sure he knew he was forgiven, Peter felt ashamed of himself. That's why he was clothed.

We all try to put on our best spiritual face when we are around other Christians. We want to cover our weaknesses. If fancy religious clothes aren't enough to do the job, we will throw ourselves in the sea to keep from letting people see who we really are.

A Journey Through The Gospels

Many Bible teachers have made a big deal out of the different words for love that Jesus and Peter use *(agape and phileo)* but I've never been able to make much spiritual headway with that.

No, to me it's clear that Jesus was just making sure that Peter knew He had to have the preeminent place in Peter's heart. The life-changing ministry Peter was called to do was not going to be easy, and Jesus tells Peter that difficult days are ahead (John 21:8).

Then Jesus says the important words, *"Follow Me."*

It's as if Jesus is saying, "All is forgiven, Peter. I chose you and I know you. The past is behind and my new path is right in front of you. It will be rough, but just keep on the path. Tend my lambs and follow Me."

This is the same message and calling that Jesus has for each of us. The times, places, and people vary. Still He asks us, "Do you love Me? Follow Me."

Let's Pray:
Jesus, I thank you for making me your disciple.
I love you, Lord, and I choose to follow you!
In your name, Amen!

100 Days With Jesus

Day 100
Hosea 6:3

Do You Know Him?

Oh, that we might know the LORD! Let us press on to know Him. He will respond to us as surely as the arrival of dawn or the coming of rains in early spring. - Hosea 6:3 NLT

Henry walked down the long hallway to his Sunday school class. It was his first Sunday in church, and he was headed to a men's class. He greeted the eight other fellows there, and they welcomed him warmly. The leader asked him to say a little bit about himself. He told them about his profession as a cabinet maker and a little about his family, but then he told them about Ruth.

"If you really want to know about me you should ask my wife, Ruth sometime. We've been married for 34 years, and there is not a day goes by that I don't thank the Lord for that. Next to following Jesus, Ruthie is the best thing that's ever happened to me. I could say all the things that guys normally say about their wife, but there is more: Ruth knows me.

"Ruth knows what makes me tick. She knows what gets my juices flowing. If there is a problem up the road I'm headed for, Ruthie sees it way ahead of me. When I get out of whack about something, it's Ruth that pulls me back to square. She is as beautiful as the day I met her. She is my inspiration. She is the sunny day in my rainy week. She is the music of my life."

Henry stopped and there was a bit of an uncomfortable silence in

A Journey Through The Gospels

the room. Guys don't usually talk like that to each other. The leader recognized how much Henry had shared his heart and put himself out there. He simply smiled at Henry and said, "I can't wait to meet Ruth."

———————

When someone asks us about our faith in Christ, do we share a bible verse and leave it at that? Do we tell our story of salvation and stop? Or do we bring a sense of a vibrant relationship, a friend and a brother. Do we introduce them to the lover of our soul?

Do you know Jesus? If not, you can begin that relationship today. Simply recognize your need for a Savior, confess your sins, open the door of your heart and invite Him to come in as Lord. He will rush in to meet you!

Perhaps you've known Jesus for a long time, but you don't talk about Him the way Henry talked about Ruth. God wants you to know there is more. When Henry got married to Ruth, their relationship didn't stop there. It grew and grew, becoming richer and deeper and more faceted. They went through the mountains and the valleys together.

Jesus is calling you up higher. Rush to meet Him. There is more to Him than you know. And, like Ruthie, people you meet will want to meet Him too.

Let's Pray:
Lord, you are my life! I want to set aside everything
to know and love you more. Share your heart with me today.
In your name, Amen!

Cornerstone Television Network

We're Here for You!

*L*ooking to grow even more in your walk with Jesus?

Here at Cornerstone Television, we're excited to share God's Word with you through original television programs (produced right here in Pittsburgh, PA), national teaching programs, and our 24-hour prayer line.

- WATCH ONLINE AT CTVN.ORG

- Sign up for daily e-devotionals delivered right to your inbox: CTVN.org/devo

- Follow us on social media:
    - /cornerstonetv
    - /cornerstonetv
    - /cornerstonetelevision

Cornerstone Television Network is a 501(c)(3) nonprofit committed to sharing the Gospel through Christian media. To partner with our ministry, visit ctvn.org or mail to: 1 Signal Hill Drive, Wall, PA 15148.

CornerStone
TELEVISION NETWORK

Need Prayer?

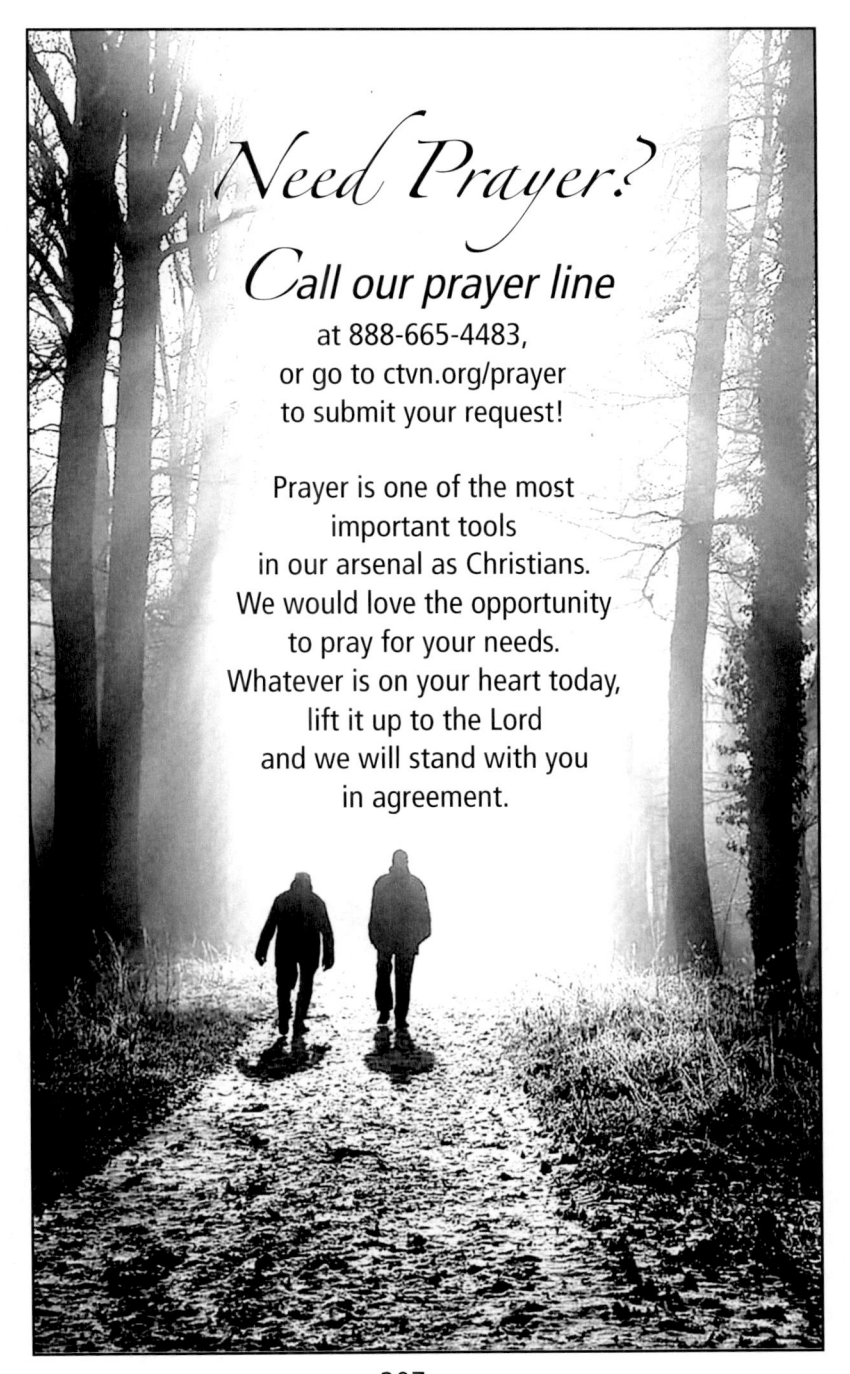

Call our prayer line
at 888-665-4483,
or go to ctvn.org/prayer
to submit your request!

Prayer is one of the most
important tools
in our arsenal as Christians.
We would love the opportunity
to pray for your needs.
Whatever is on your heart today,
lift it up to the Lord
and we will stand with you
in agreement.

Acknowledgements

First, all praise to Jesus, our Lord. It is He who put this project in my heart, and put others in my life to draw it out.

The initial encouragement for this project came from Amanda Brougher. In her role as Prayer Partner Coordinator, she knew that our prayer partners would need spiritual nourishment as they had to work from home during a remodeling of our Ministry Center. This devotional began as emails to those wonderful prayer warriors. All of them were gracious and encouraging. Joy Anna Rosendale especially, and emphatically, encouraged me with calls and notes.

Special thanks to Steve Johnson, CEO of Cornerstone Television, for his encouragement when I offered this devotional to our ministry. His suggestions and continued support became the project's catalyst.

Mary Anne Skeba served as the creative director for this project, and her work is on every page. With grace and the creative spark of God, she brought the book through. You deserve a monument in your honor, Mary Anne! A million thanks for your work and your prayers.

Many thanks to Crystal Bynum, Marketing Director at Cornerstone, for her ideas and project management skills, and for putting her team on the case. Tons of kudos to my proofreaders: Mary Anne Zulisky, Amanda Gaines Borders, and Anna Frye all read and re-read the manuscript. Who knew how much dissension there could be about my lack of use of commas! Anna spearheaded the final stages of the book, and she and Amanda also gave important layout input. My daughter, Ashley Miller, helped with proofing, too, and gave input on the cover and title.

To my family, Andrew, Tiffany, Ashley, spouses and grandkids: Thank you for your patience in allowing me to use you as occasional examples in this book. God has used each of you to teach me what it means to be a dad and a Christian.

Finally, thanks to Jean. She was my favorite "test audience," and got to hear the entries before anyone else, providing honest feedback and lots of encouragement. Honey, our relationship began with a walk, where we talked about Jesus, and that's never changed. Sounds like a good idea for a book!